NAPLES AND SURROUNDING AREA

Editions KINA ITALIA

Introduction

Theories on the foundation of Naples are obscure and controversial. Historians and archeologists agree that the city is of Greek origin and that colonists from nearby Cumae dug its first foundations. But the details of this event are not clear. Some believe that Neapolis was the "new city," created in opposition to an "old city" (Paleopolis), while others refute the existence of an older inhabited settlement and assert that during the sixth century B.C. the Cumaeans directly founded a Neapolis which is now located between present-day Via Foria and the sea. Whatever its origins, the choice of location for its establishment was certainly fortunate. With a wonderful climate, luxuriant nature and an enchanting view of one of the most beautiful gulfs in the world, in Roman times Naples began to expand and acquire the fame it would maintain unchanged over the centuries, centuries of a complex and tormented history consisting of brief periods of prosperous independence and hundreds of years of foreign domination, both benevolent and illuminated and otherwise. Byzantines, Goths, Normans, Swabians, Angevins, Aragons and Bourbons: the city retains at least traces of them all, and in many cases much more. Romulus Augustulus, Tancred, Frederick II, Charles I of Anjou, Johanna I, Ferdinand I of Aragon, Philip II of Habsburg, the viceroy Don Pedro of Toledo, and Joachim Murat: all of them held Naples and Naples was forced to submit to their munificence and their folly, their benevolence and their cruelty, their politics and their vendettas. Nearly all of them gave the city grandiose monuments and tyranny, sumptuous churches and battles, useful public works and burdensome taxes. On this roller coaster ride of feast and famine, poverty and wealth, peace and war punctuated by natural disasters

of every sort, Naples never gave up one fundamental aspect: its independence. Even when foreign domination was at its height, the city was never totally subdued. Suffice it to note the popular uprisings that dot its history, the famous revolt by the populist Masaniello, and the assaults on the centers of contested power. But apart from these frequent episodes, there has always been a more intimate, sometimes intellectual independence in every Neopolitan, often experienced in the depth of the soul, in silence, rather than as a chorus of shouts in the square. It is almost as if for centuries, from generation to generation, Neopolitans have passed down the duty of preserving their freedom, that character that can only be defined as "Neopolitan." Nothing else can explain the constant cultural liveliness and intellectual freedom of this city, its entrepreneurship and unlimited energy, its humanity, its pride and its ability to overcome each of the thousand events that have marked its history.
Naples is an art city in the true sense of the word, a city where art seems to spring up spontaneously from the fertile earth, producing wonders in every area, from painting to music, poetry to architecture, theater to dance. Its roads are strewn with splendid and grandiose monuments, and with the people that daily "make" Naples, perpetuating its culture and its inimitable way of life, sometimes criticized and often misunderstood but always admired in at least one of its innumerable forms. Neapolis, truly a city that is always new, a metropolis of the year 2000 where one can still breathe its ancient and deep culture and feel the genuineness of its people, unchanged over the centuries.

First Part

Piazza Municipio

A lively administrative and commercial center of the city, this gently sloping square, refurbished and beautified for the G7 meeting in 1994, is an elegant parlor for admiring some of the principal beauties of Naples. From the vast center area, adorned with the solemn monument to Victor Emmanuel II (built in the 19th century by the Campanian sculptors Tommaso Solari and Alfonso Balzico), it is in fact possible to see not only the nearby Palazzo del Municipio and the San Giacomo degli Spagnoli church (which directly face the square), but also Castel Nuovo (also known as the Maschio Angioino, or Angevin Keep), the Palazzo Reale, the port area and, in the distance, Vesuvius to one side and the green hill of San Martino to the other, where the white building of the San Martino Carthusian monastery and Castel Sant'Elmo stand out. To the west, the imposing Palazzo del Municipio, also known as San Giacomo due to the adjoining church dedicated to the saint, was constructed based on a design by the Neopolitan architects Luigi and Stefano Gasse in 1816-1825 in order to house the ministries of the Bourbon reign. The right wing of the building is occupied by the San Giacomo degli Spagnoli church, thus called because it was commissioned by the viceroy Don Pedro of Toledo. It dates back to 1540, but its current appearance is due to a series of transformations made about two hundred years later, around the middle of the 18th century. The interior, with a Latin cross plan, three naves preceded by a vestibule and a wide apse, is full of artistic works, most of which date back to the 16th century, in particular paintings and sculptures that decorate the tombs. The most notable of these is the sepulcher of Don Pedro of Toledo, adorned with statues of the cardinal virtues, with relief work on the base depicting historical episodes in the life of the city. Leaving the Palazzo del Municipio and going toward the sea, one sees the Mercadante theater on the left, constructed in 1778 but with the main façade redone in the late 19th century. In the port area at the end of the square stretches the broad Molo Angioino, built in 1302 by order of Charles II of Anjou and which separates the Bacino Angioino, commissioned in the late 16th century by the then viceroy, from the Porto Mercantile, built by Charles II of Anjou and later expanded and completed by subsequent rulers.

1

2

3

1) Piazza Municipio and Castel Sant'Elmo
2) Piazza Municipio
3) Piazza Municipio - Fountains
4) Maschio Angioino (Angevin Keep)
5) Entrance to the gardens of Palazzo Reale

4

5

Maschio Angioino

This building is located south of the Piazza del Municipio on a rise that makes its bulk even more imposing and majestic. Known as Castel Nuovo in order to differentiate it from the older Castel dell'Ovo and Castel Capuano, it was christened the Maschio Angioino (the Angevin Keep) in reference to its founder, Charles I of Anjou, who had it built between 1279 and 1282 as his residence. Nevertheless, Alfonso of Aragon had it almost completely rebuilt by Spanish and Tuscan craftsmen and artists in order to repair the enormous damage the building suffered during the wars that bloodied the reign during the 15th century (the principal remaining feature of the original building is the Palatina chapel, which now houses sculptures and frescoes from the 14th and 15th centuries belonging to the Museo Civico; paintings from the 15th to the 20th centuries and silver and bronzes from the Museum are contained on the three floors in the south wing of the castle). During the first half of the 16th century the circular exterior ramparts, which had been built a few years earlier by the Florentine Antonio da Settignano especially for housing the artillery of the Aragon king, were replaced with

1) Detail from the portal of the Maschio Angioino
2) Maschio Angioino (Angevin Keep)

1

2

Spanish ramparts (one of which was completely destroyed in 1536 when the gunpowder stored there exploded), but the major renovations and the most important changes in the structure were made in the 18th century. Finally, in the early 20th century extensive restoration and partial reconstruction based in part on ancient documents that depicted it have given the Maschio Angioino its present-day appearance.

Galleria Umberto I

To the right along the elegant Via San Carlo from the Piazza del Municipio, one encounters the monumental building, one of the most majestic in Italy, named after King Umberto I. The imposing edifice, added to the city structure as a connecting gallery in accordance with a common 19th century plan, was constructed between 1887 and 1891 by the Neopolitan Emanuele Rocco, with the assistance of other architects. Resting on a wide octagonal base, the showy cupola designed by Paolo Boubée, with an iron supporting structure and covered in glass (as is the entire gallery), fully 57.5 meters high at its vertex, gives the building a remarkable lightness that blends perfectly with the airy fanlights and gallery wings. The beautifully ornamented inside walls are divided into two upper levels resting on pillars on the ground floor, while the ornamentation on the exterior of the gallery is

3

abundant and grandiloquent. A circular hall, richly decorated in belle époque style motifs, was excavated below the structure in order to create the Teatro Margherita.

Piazza Trieste e Trento

Coming out of the Galleria Umberto I and proceeding along Via San Carlo again, one comes upon this small ornate square with a beautiful fountain in the center. In the past it was known as the Piazza San Ferdinando due to the presence of the San Ferdinando church with its façade inserted into the irregular plan of the square. The church, constructed and immediately modified in the 17th century, originally belonged to the Jesuits, who dedicated it to St. Francis Xavier, and only in the second half of the 18th century was it given its present name in honor of King Ferdinand Bourbon. This explains why most of the paintings in the single nave interior depict St. Francis Xavier and not St. Ferdinand, who is nevertheless present on the main altar in a 19th century painting by the Neopolitan Filippo Maldarelli.

1-4) Galleria Umberto I
2) Piazza Trieste e Trento
3) Entrance to the Galleria Umberto I

4

.LFIERRO
SEIKO
Dr. G. CAUTIERO
BAR GIUSTO

1

1) Teatro San Carlo
2) Teatro San Carlo: interior

Teatro San Carlo

On the corner between the Piazza Trieste e Trento and Via San Carlo stands one of the most grandiose and fortunate works ever built in Naples during the reign of King Charles Bourbon. The Teatro San Carlo, second in Italy only to La Scala in Milan (constructed only forty years later and which can lay mutual claim to having one of the best ballet schools in Italy), is also one of the most celebrated and important temples of lyric opera in the world. The building that houses it was very rapidly (in only eight months) constructed in 1737 based on a design by the Sicilian architect Giovanni Antonio Medrano and was immediately opened on November 4 of the same year for the king's name day, with a performance of a work by Metastasio. Later modified and further embellished (the atrium and loggia of the façade date to the first decade of the 19th century), the hall was completely destroyed by a fire in February 1816. The reconstruction work was just as rapid as the original construction, and in the summer of the same year the Florentine Antonio Niccolini, who was in charge of the reconstruction work, was able to give the city its most famous theater back. Other restoration and modernizing work followed until the beginning of the 20th century, when the roof of the edifice was raised and the large stage (about 33 x 34 meters in size) and fittings were given a new look. Inside, the rich gilt ornamentation of the hall, which seats three thousand spectators, is awe-inspiring and prompted Stendahl to state, "One's first impression is that one has stumbled onto the palace of an Oriental emperor. (...)" Nevertheless, it does not affect the sober elegance of the whole, domi-

2

nated by the majestic royal box crowned by 184 other boxes located on seven levels, adorned by balustrades with elaborate decorative motifs. The vault is embellished by a fresco with a mythological scene depicting Minerva and the greatest Greek, Latin and Italian poets. The nineteenth century scene (Homer and the Muses with bards and musicians) that appears on the curtain is also mythological. Famous worldwide for its perfect acoustics, the San Carlo hall in Naples has hosted premiers of numerous famous works, including La Sonnambula by Vincenzo Bellini.

Piazza del Plebiscito and the Pizzofalcone district

1) San Francesco di Paola church seen from the Palazzo Reale

Proceed from the Piazza Trieste e Trento along the wall of the Palazzo Reale that faces the area, until reaching the nearby Piazza del Plebiscito. Grandiose, with its vast rectangular square at the foot of Mount Echia (known as Pizzofalcone until the 13th century), its western boundaries are marked by the splendid semi-elliptical arcade begun in 1809 by Leopoldo Laperuta at the request of the viceroy Joachim Murat. At its center, the Doric colonnade showily frames the solemn main façade of its near contemporary, the San Francesco di Paola basilica (see below), in front of which are the two equestrian statues of Ferdinand I (who commissioned the church) and Charles III of Bourbon, created respectively by the sculptors Antonio Calì and the more famous Antonio Canova. The Neopolitan Laperuta is responsible for the structure of the Palazzo della Prefettura (1815), at the far north end of the square. On the south end, at the corner of Via Cesario Console, is the Palazzo Salerno, built at the end of the 18th century.
The area across from the arcade is entirely occupied by the imposing bulk of the Palazzo Reale (see below), with its original 17th century façade 170 meters in length.
The western side of the square opens out to the characteristic Pizzofalcone district, thus called because of the name of the hill on which it stands, all that remains of the ancient volcanic crater of Mt. Echia. The hillock, famous in Latin times for the splendid Lucullo villa that stood there, was first transformed into a fortified town around the middle of the 1st century A.D., then became the site of cenobies, monastic buildings and churches and in the 14th century again took on a defensive and military aspect under Alfonso I of Aragon, who erected a fortress there. The district's urban development took place primarily between the 16th and 17th centuries, when numerous houses and sumptuous residential buildings were constructed. Between 1927 and 1930 the Galleria della Vittoria tunnel was excavated under the rise; it is an imposing work of engineering over six hundred meters long and connects the eastern part of the city with the western half. Turning right from the Piazza del Plebiscito at the Palazzo Salerno, a ramp leads to the Piazzetta Salazar, where the Istituto d'Arte (1878) has a small museum that contains an interesting collection of applied art with valuable items from various periods, from the splendid Oriental cloths of the 5th century to the refined eighteenth century products of Capodimonte make. From here, entering Via Solitaria on the left and Via Egiziaca a Pizzofalcone on the right (where the 17th century church of Santa Maria Egiziaca a Pizzofalcone stands with its splendid marble ornamentation inside, as well as the 16th century Palazzo Carafa di San Severino), and proceeding down Via Nunziatella, one comes to the Nunziatella building on Via Parisi, dating back to 1588, with the adjoining 18th century church which contains precious paintings and sculptures. Going back along Via Parisi and turning right, one enters the elegant Via Monte di Dio, along which stand

2) Piazza Plebiscito: equestrian monument

Page 16/17: night view of Piazza Plebiscito and the Palazzo Reale

some of the most beautiful courtly buildings of the 18th century. Particularly noteworthy for its ornamentation and original internal furnishings is the Palazzo Serra di Cassano, designed by the Neopolitan architect Ferdinando Sanfelice.
At the end of the street on the left in the square bearing the same name is the church of Santa Maria degli Angeli a Pizzofalcone, with the beautiful baroque façade dominated by the majestic cupola. Built in the early 17th century by the Tuscan Francesco Grimaldi, its three nave interior flanked by side chapels holds interesting paintings by Luca Giordano (Holy Family and San Giordano) and the grandiose ornamentation of the cupola depicting Paradise. Following Via Gennaro Serra from the Piazza Santa Maria degli Angeli, one arrives at the Piazza Carolina, right next to the Palazzo della Prefettura, and from here one can return to the Piazza del Plebiscito.

2

Palazzo Reale

Built as a residence for the viceroy Fernandez Ruiz de Castro, Count of Lemos, and designed by the Ticino architect Domenico Fontana between 1600 and 1602, the imposing palace occupies a large area between Via San Carlo, Via Parco del Castello, Via Ammiraglio Acton and the Piazza del Plebiscito, which its majestic façade overlooks. The building was extended and remodeled both during the mid-18th century and, particularly its interior, in the early 19th century. In 1837 it was damaged in a fire and was restored by the architect Gaetano Genovese upon order of Ferdinand II, with notable changes made in its southern façade. New restoration work was then necessary in order to remedy further and more serious damage to the palace due to bombing during the Second World War.
Along with the inside courtyard of honor, the main façade, divided into two levels overlooking the arcade on the ground floor, is the only remaining element from the original 17th century structure.
The arcade was nevertheless partially remodeled by Luigi Vanvitelli in the mid-18th century, transforming

1) Entrance to the Palazzo Reale
2) Palazzo Reale: the façade

2

1

2

3

4

5

some of the arches into niches by closing them and giving the arcade its present day appearance with alternating filled and empty spaces. The eight niches formed remained empty until 1888, when Umberto I decided to place eight statues in them, created by contemporary sculptors and depicting the greatest rulers of Naples. From the left, in spatial and chronological order, appear Roger the Norman, Frederick II of Swabia, Charles I of Anjou, Alfonso I of Aragon, Charles V, Charles III of Bourbon, the viceroy Joachim Murat and Victor Emmanuel II of Savoy. From the main entrance on the Piazza del Plebiscito one enters the large, square courtyard of honor, designed by Domenico Fontana in the 17th century and embellished by the arcade and overlooking loggia. The famous bronze door located in the atrium was originally found in the lower arch of the Arco di Trionfo of Castel Nuovo. The work (1462-1468) was commissioned to Guglielmo Monaco of Paris by Ferdinand I in order to celebrate his victory over John of Anjou and rebel barons. The important episodes of the affair are depicted on six beauti-

1) Palazzo Reale: detail of the stairway
2) West passageway
3) Coaches Court with its fountain
4) Flower box detail: Capodimonte ceramic (Hercules Hall)
5) Hercules Hall: detail of the ceiling
6) Palazzo Reale: Throne Room

1

ful panels sculpted in bas-relief that adorn the door. The monumental staircase of honor, constructed in the mid-17th century but altered and embellished with new, extremely rich decorations in multicolored marble during the restoration work done by Genovese between 1838 and 1842, starts from the atrium and reaches the first floor, where the historic Apartment is located.
The viceroy and the kings of the Bourbon dynasty lived here until the fire of 1837, when they moved to the upper floor. After visiting the Court Theater one enters the Museum, located in the grandiose, richly decorated hall containing period furniture, paintings and objects, in some cases brought here from the Tuileries in Paris by order of Joachim Murat and Caroline Bonaparte.
The Palazzo Reale also houses the extensive Biblioteca Nazionale di Napoli, a library open to the public

2

3

1) Palazzo Reale: Diplomatic Room
2) Hercules Hall: Atlas
3) Palazzo Reale: Gran Capitano Hall - fresco by A. Vaccaro
4) Hercules Hall: three vases in ceramic and brass
5) Capodimonte clock
6) Joachim Murat's studio
7) Door in Pompeian style

4

5

6

7

since 1804. Developed around an original core of works (the Farnese collection transferred to Naples by Charles Bourbon when he ascended the throne), it was gradually expanded through acquisitions of very important works, including the Herculaneum papyruses of Officina, consisting of about two thousand papyruses found in the Officina Villa in Herculaneum during excavations in 1752. Its precious heritage includes manuscripts from the 3rd century, Gospel books from the 5th to the 9th centuries, 15th and 16th century illuminated codices, 15th century incunabula, antique books, letters and rare documents.

San Francesco di Paola

Right in front of the Palazzo Reale, on the other side of the large Piazza del Plebiscito, is the majestic basilica of San Francesco di Paola, crowned by the grand semicircular arcade supported by Doric columns, commissioned by Joachim Murat in the early 19th century.
The church (begun in 1817 and not completed until 1846) was commissioned by Ferdinand I of Bourbon, who, as indicated in the inscription on its façade, had it erected in order to thank the saint for helping him regain his reign, sanctioned on May 20, 1815 in the Treaty of Catalanza. Due to a strange coincidence, or perhaps a carefully planned design, the architecture of this splendid whole unites the intentions of two men who in life were strenuously opposed to each other.
Pietro Bianchi of Ticino, the author of the work, was greatly inspired by the Roman Pantheon for the architecture of the basilica, covered by the large cupola erected on the imposing tambour and preceded by an elegant pronaos resting on six central columns and two side pillars in Ionian style surmounted by a triangular tympanum in the center of which stands the statue of Religion flanked by those of St. Ferdinand of Castille and St. Francesco of Paola.
Passing through the entry atrium, the sides of which open out to two chapels, one reaches the splendid inner rotunda, surrounded by a colonnade of 34 marble columns in Corinthian style and an equal number of pillars around them.
The large space (fully 34 meters in diameter) is showily surmounted by the cupola, which is 53 meters high from the ground to the vertex.
The main altar, facing the entry, with its splendid ornamentation in precious and semiprecious stones, was constructed during the mid-17th century by the Neopolitan Fra Anselmo Cangiano for the Santi Apostoli church, from which it was then brought here.
The basilica's interior walls are embellished with eight statues constructed by various 19th century artists. Of particular note are those of the four Evangelists and the group depicting St. Francesco of Paola receiving the insignia of charity from an angel. In the apse, of note is the painting by the Roman Vincenzo Camuccini depicting St. Francesco of Paola resurrecting a dead man.

1

2

1-3) San Francesco di Paola church seen from the Palazzo Reale
2) Piazza Plebiscito and San Francesco di Paola church

3

D·O·M·D·FRANCISCO·DE·PAVLA·FERDINANDVS·I·EX·VOTO·A

Second Part

1

2

1) Immacolata Fountain
2) Borgo Marinaro
3) Castel dell'Ovo

From Santa Lucia a Mare to Borgo Marinaro

From the Piazza del Plebiscito, turning left after the Palazzo Salerno, one enters Via Cesare Console, which descends toward the sea and soon crosses Via Santa Lucia. The road, which was once lined with the modest homes of fishermen, was modernized and expanded as early as the 17th century, after which it became one of the most frequented and pleasant streets in Naples. Going along it, to the almost immediate left one may see the small church of Santa Lucia a Mare, which name is owed to the fact that at the time of its construction (which was almost certainly shortly before the 9th century despite the popular tradition that it was built as early as the reign of Emperor Constantine) it was located at the edge of the sea. The original building was replaced by a new chapel in the late 16th century, and this was just the beginning of a series of unfortunate remodeling work on the church. In fact, in the mid-19th century, the 16th century church was replaced by a new structure, which was then replaced by the present structure after being destroyed during the Second World War. Although the outside architecture has not retained its historical characteristics, the interior holds precious works of ancient art. Of particular note is an arc-shaped painting from the Neopolitan school depicting a Rosary, dating back to the time of the second church (second half of the 16th century). The moving wooden statue of St. Lucia, also of the Neopolitan school, is from the 18th century.

Going back up Via S. Lucia and entering Via Cesario Console on the right again, one may proceed to the sea where, near the intersection with the parallel Via Ammiraglio Acton, beautified by the green public gardens, there is a statue of Emperor Augustus (1936). From here, again turning right, one enters the seaside promenade on Via Nazario Sauro. Along this walk, which is extremely pleasant due to the spectacular views of the city and the open sea, stands a monument to Umberto I completed in 1910 by the Neopolitan sculptor Achille D'Orsi. The road ends with the Immacolatella fountain, located in one of the most scenic areas of the city. Dating back to the early 17th century, the marble monument consists of three arches (the central one is higher than those to the sides) heavily ornamented by statues, caryatids and other decorative elements.

Via Partenope, which almost immediately intersects with the Borgo Marinaro jetty area on the left, begins after the fountain. Facing the small Santa Lucia port, the neighborhood stands on a rocky promontory and is one of the most characteristic areas of traditional Naples, still maintaining folk rhythms and customs that are now difficult to find in other parts of the city. The cheerful charm of Borgo Marinaro is a stark contrast to the cold and imposing jetty of one of the primary Neopolitan fortresses,

Castel dell'Ovo, with its legendary name, a witness and heir to centuries of Neopolitan history. Borgo Marinaro can also be reached from the Santa Lucia church by going

3

down Via Santa Lucia, which intersects with Via Chiatamone before turning into Via Partenope.
In ancient times this street was scattered with grottos, inhabited even in prehistoric times, which were closed by order of the viceroy Pedro of Toledo in the 16th century.

Castel dell'Ovo

The massive fortress that stands on the islet of Borgo Marinaro probably owes its name to its ovoid design. However, there is an evocative Neopolitan legend, possibly dating from the 14th century, that traces the castle's name to Virgil, the great Latin poet who in the Dark Ages was also considered a sorcerer and who is said to have bound the fate of the castle to a fragile egg he had closed up in a carafe; if the egg broke, the castle would collapse. In reality, the building, which was originally built in 1128 on a site formerly occupied by a monastery (numerous traces of which have been found during restoration work), proved to be quite solid and robust until at least the end of the 15th century, when luck truly seemed to desert it. The castle, witness to much splendor, intrigue and suffering (Conradin of Swabia and the two young sons of Manfred were imprisoned here until their deaths, as was Queen Johanna I), was first bombed by Charles VIII, then destroyed by an explosive device. Almost completely restored in the late 17th century, it was bombed again in 1733, this time by the troops of Charles Bourbon. Visitors to the building can see the various remodeling work and extensions completed over the centuries, from the oldest, ordered by Frederick II (addition of the towers) to those from the 19th century. In addition to the architectural elements typical of fortified structures, numerous vestiges of monastic life that had continued for centuries remain within the castle. The remains of the 7th century San Salvatore church are evocative, as are the monastic cells dug into the rock and the large hall of columns that was probably the monastery refectory, with arches supported by marble columns dating from Roman times.

Via Caracciolo

Leaving the Castel dell'Ovo and the islet of Borgo Marinaro, turn left onto Via Partenope and follow it to the evocative Piazza della Vittoria, which offers splendid views of the city and the hill where the Carthusian monastery stands. Behind the flower beds that embellish it, on the corner of Via Gaetani, one can visit the 17th century church of Santa Maria della Vittoria, enclosed within a building and erected in gratitude to the Virgin for the 1571 victory in the battle of Lepanto. Nearly half of the scenic walk down Via Partenope and

1

2

1) Castel dell'Ovo
2) Piazza Vittoria
3) Via Caracciolo

3

Via Caracciolo is dominated by the Villa Comunale and its enormous park shaded by palms, eucalyptus and other trees. The estate was opened to the public around the end of the 18th century upon order of Ferdinand IV, who gave architect Carlo Vanvitelli, the son of the more famous Luigi, the task of transforming the area into a garden. From the early 19th century until the 20th century the park was further enlarged and beautified until it assumed its present appearance. The large avenue immersed in luxuriant vegetation is scattered with statues, monuments (an excellent example is the one erected in 1936 in honor of Armando Diaz) and fountains from various periods (including one with a basin that comes from the Paestum excavations), and also contains a number of 19th century buildings such as the music kiosk, the Circolo della Stampa building and a small Ionian temple. The actual villa, in the center of the park, is home to an important Neopolitan institution founded in 1872 by the German naturalist Antonio Dohrn, the Stazione Zoologica, devoted to the study of marine flora and fauna.

Villa Pignatelli

The sumptuous residence is the most important monument facing the Riviera di Chiaia. Built in a neoclassical form by the Neopolitan Pietro Valente during the first half of the 19th century, it was purchased by the princes of Aragon Pignatelli Cortes around the end of the century and became one of the major artistic and literary salons in the city. Today owned by the State, it houses the Principe di Aragona Pignatelli Cortes Museum. Its various rooms (the Blue Room, the Music Room and the verandah atrium are particularly beautiful) with their original style furnishings (with precious examples from the 19th century, as well as mirrors and elegant furniture) provide a backdrop for the excellent 18th and 19th century paintings (numerous portraits), splendid porcelain from the major European manufacturers, sculptures, Chinese vases and luxurious furnishings that testify to the wealth and taste of its 19th century owners. In the splendid garden, where numerous exotic plants grow, is the Museo delle Carrozze, which traces the history of Italian, English and French carriages with interesting period examples.

1

2

1) Villa Pignatelli
2) Piazza della Repubblica
3) Piazza Sannazzaro
4) Panorama and Via Caracciolo
5) The "Finestrella" at Marechiaro

3

4

5

Riviera di Chiaia

In addition to the Villa Pignatelli and the Villa Comunale, other elegant buildings built in the 18th and 19th centuries line the Riviera di Chiaia. Near the Piazza della Repubblica there is the interesting San Giuseppe a Chiaia church (17th century), with its interior decorated with valuable paintings. A little farther on, Via Santa Maria al Portico to the left leads to the church of the same name, also from the 17th century, with its precious frescoes by Luca Giordano.

Mergellina

Via Mergellina begins at the Piazza della Repubblica. After opening into the square dedicated to the poet Iacopo Sannazzaro (1458-1530) it reaches the sea at the Mergellina inlet, at the foot of the Posillipo hill. With the small Sannazzaro port, full of fishermen and tourists, and the cable car station for Posillipo, it is one of the most beautiful and characteristic areas of Naples. Here stands the small Santa Maria del Parto church, commissioned by Sannazzaro. The building holds the humanist's tomb, constructed in 1537 and adorned with sculptures and bas-reliefs. The church's pictorial decoration is unusual due to the juxtaposition of Christian and Pagan themes, well illustrated by the composition with Abraham and the Angels next to Venus and Mercury, and the depiction of Astronomy with the Lower Arts (philosophy, grammar and rhetoric).

Posillipo

Famous for its marvelous natural beauties, Posillipo is located halfway between the Gulf of Naples and that of Pozzuoli. Via Posillipo runs through it, with splendid villas immersed in luxuriant gardens, monuments (including the 17th century fountain of Neptune and the votive altar to the Fallen Patriots, established in the late 19th century), and above all the unforgettable views of the city and the gulf (especially from Cape Posillipo). At the end of Via Posillipo, at the so-called Cape crossroads, by following the little Via Marechiaro one arrives at the district of the same name, located in an enviable position, with its picturesque charm of a fishing village still intact. Those who want the most spectacular panorama can reach the Posillipo park from the crossroads, flanked by two gulfs at the end of a promontory. The surrounding area contains interesting traces of the Roman era Villa Pausilypon (literally "that eases pain").

Nisida

For good reason called Nesis (little island) by the ancient Greeks, the nearly circular island with a perimeter of only about 2 kilometers is actually a volcanic crater. It can easily be reached by crossing the bridge which connects it to solid land at Coroglio, near the Posillipo park. With part of it containing vineyards, it still has a large building dating back to the Anjevin period which was used by the Bourbons to jail political prisoners.

Fuorigrotta

This district stands at the entrance of the Galleria IV Giornate, a tunnel about one kilometer long excavated in 1940 under the Posillipo hill which comes out at the other side near the so-called Tomb of Virgil (in reality an Augustinian-era columbarium).
Developed between 1950 and 1970, the densely populated area thick with modern housing is intersected by large roads that the city planning of the time attempted to integrate with the surrounding environment and camouflage by interposing flower beds and trees, in an effort to prevent the neighborhood from looking like a classic "concrete jungle." The neighborhood's center of attraction is without doubt the San Paolo stadium, a large athletic facility opened in December 1959 which attracts thousands of soccer fans. But apart from the athletic facility,

1) Nisida: night view
2) Polytechnic

3

Fuorigrotta also contains the important Mostra d'Oltremare, a true district within a district.

The vast area (now over 600,000 square meters in size) was originally created in 1939-40 in order to showcase the successes of fascist Italy in the African colonies; in the early 1950's after the end of the Second World War, during which it suffered enormous damage, it was specially rebuilt to host fairs, special shows and athletic and artistic activities. In addition to the over twenty exhibition pavilions there are theaters, an Olympic-size swimming pool, tennis courts, greenhouses and a vast multifunctional playing field.

4

5

3-4) San Paolo Stadium
5) Racetrack

Third Part

Via Toledo

This street, which begins at the Piazza Trieste e Trento, owes its name to the viceroy Pedro of Toledo, the Marquis of Villafranca, who ordered its construction in 1536 with the idea of creating a new noble settlement in the area. The project was a great success, and around the elegant buildings that were built, lower class neighborhoods soon arose as well, which the so-called Spanish quarters most faithfully represent. Created in the mid-16th century and now one of the most characteristic and in some ways controversial areas of the city, this neighborhood above the street, where many typical aspects of the Neopolitan "philosophy of daily life" have survived progress and urbanization, has in fact succeeded in preserving its original style, with a thick network of densely populated streets. Going past the side entrance of the Galleria Umberto I, a short distance from the elegant Palazzo Berio (erected in 1772 by Luigi Vanvitelli) and the cable car station for Vomero, and turning right onto Via Santa Brigida one finds the Santa Brigida church. Dating back to the mid-17th century, the building holds valuable paintings by Luca Giordano, including the Apotheosis of St. Brigida in the cupola, a true masterpiece of perspective painting. Farther along Via Toledo and recog-nizable by its majestic marble fa-çade, the imposing Palazzo del Banco di Napoli (1939) rises on the right, the first bank founded in Italy. Again on the right, the Rione Carità district is located behind other sumptuous buildings. It was opened around 1950 based on a hotly disputed city planning scheme that required the demolition of numerous historic buildings in order to create a new area in decided contrast to the surrounding zone. To the left of the beginning of Via Diaz, where the Banca Nazionale del Lavoro building stands on the corner, is the Santa Maria delle Grazie church, originally from the 17th century but redone in the 19th century. A short detour on this side leads to the interesting churches of Montecalvario (16th century, with a splendid majolica floor added during 19th century

1

2

restoration work) and Santa Maria della Concezione (18th century). Going back to Via Toledo and passing the Piazza della Carità with its church of the same name (redone in the early 20th century but of 16th century origin), there is another church, San Nicola, which holds a small treas-ure of 17th century Neopolitan paintings. Of special note are the beautiful works by Francesco Solimena. From here, turning right on Via Caravita one reaches the Piazza Monteoliveto, where one of the most famous monuments in this area and the entire city is located, the Sant'Anna dei Lombardi church. Almost at the end of Via Toledo, on the right, the façade of the Palazzo Maddaloni (1582) preserves a magnificent 17th century portal, with lovely frescoes by the Neopolitan painter Fedele Fischetti (18th century) in the sumptuous halls. At this point Via Toledo crosses a portion of "Spaccanapoli" (Via Scura to the left and Via Capitelli to the right), the long and very lively straight road that symbolically "splits" the city in half from east to west.

Sant'Anna dei Lombardi

Also known as the church of Monteoliveto, construction was begun in 1411, but it was then greatly changed in the 17th century and restored after the Second World War after suffering grave damage from bombings. Its name commemorates the fact that in the mid-19th century it and the adjoining monastery were ceded to the brother-hood of Sant'Anna dei Lombardi, which church had been destroyed in an earthquake. The Olivetani convent (founded at the same time) long held the favor of the Aragons, who greatly contributed to its adornment (Giorgio Vasari was in charge of decorating one room, where as in the church, he painted excellent frescoes) and enrichment, donating it a precious library of codes. The building, which originally included four cloisters adorned with gardens and fountains, was closed in 1799 and

1) Sant'Anna dei Lombardi church: nave and organ
2) Vestry
3) Via Monteoliveto, Gravina Palace and fountain
4) Avalos Chapel
5) Mourning for Christ, by Guido Mazzoni, sculptor (1492)

3

4

5

1

used for a certain period as a private residence divided into a number of living units. Passing the atrium, which opens onto a rather sober façade, one proceeds inside, to a single nave flanked by side chapels. Looking up above the entry, flanked by two altars adorned with 16th century sculptures, one sees the enormous late 17th century organ, and even farther up, the beautiful lacunar ceiling. A visit to the chapels offers a panorama of Renaissance sculpture of rare beauty and richness, so much so that some consider this church a true museum. For example, in the Correale chapel, the second on the right, one can admire an altar created by one of the major figures of 15th century sculpture, the Florentine Benedetto da Maiano, who adorned it with a refined relief of the Annunciation and with statues of St. John the Baptist and St. John Evangelist. The tomb on the right (1489) is of the founder of the chapel, Marino Curiale. In the other chapels on the right 15th century works flank 16th century paintings done by the Neopolitan Nicola Malinconico (frescoes in the vaults) and Francesco Solimena. Following the short corridor after the fifth chapel, one enters the Orefice chapel on the left, adorned with precious coloured marble. Ahead is the San Sepolcro oratory, divided into two parts, which holds tombs from the 15th century. At the end of the second room are the most beautiful and famous work in the church, the Pietà group, a work done by the Modena sculptor Guido Mazzoni. When the eight terracotta statues that comprise the group were created they were multicolored, but in the 19th century, perhaps due to the erroneous assumption that the colors were a later addition, they were "cleaned" and repainted in bronze. From here one proceeds to the Assunta chapel, with a fresco by Giorgio Vasari depicting an Olivetan monk, then to the New Sacristy (with an altar decorated with an 18th century painting), and then, ahead in the former refectory of the adjoining Olivetan monastery, the so-called Old Sacristy. The ceiling vault contains another fresco done by Giorgio Vasari in 1544, depicting Faith, Religion and Eternity, while on the walls one can admire the stall dossals, decorated with refined marquetry done almost entirely by Fra Giovanni da Verona in the early 16th century. In the rectangular apse, with an arch adorned with 17th century panels, other elegantly sculpted tombs are preserved. From here, through a small room where a 15th century Pietà is preserved, one reaches the chapels on the left, starting with the Tolosa chapel. Created by Giuliano da Maiano, the cupola pendentives are embellished with glazed terra-cotta tondi depicting the Evangelists, done by students of the Lombard Della Robbia family. Of particular note is the first chapel next to the entry, with the beautiful Nativity

2

by Antonio Rossellino da Settignano, dating back to the 1570's, the tomb of Maria of Aragon, begun by Rossellino but completed by Benedetto da Maiano, and the fresco of the Annunciation done in the style of Piero della Francesca.

Gesù Nuovo Church

To the right of the Sant'Anna dei Lombardi church (Piazza Monteoliveto), one comes to the Trinità Maggiore wharf, which leads to the Piazza del Gesù Nuovo. The church of the same name, erected during the last two decades of the 16th century, faces the square, with its center adorned by the Immacolata Spire with the gilt copper statue of the Virgin, a baroque monument of the 18th century. The façade in piperno (the gray rock found in many monuments in the city) ashlarwork, unusual for a religious building, may be explained by the fact that the church was erected on the site of a previous 15th century building and retained its main façade. The majestic baroque interior, which took fully 40 years to decorate, shows the signs of later interventions between the 17th and 19th centuries, necessary to repair damage caused by a fire and earthquake that caused the original cupola to collapse. In Greek cross form, with three naves flanked by side chapels, the church is entirely decorated in multicolored marble and invaluable paintings. Of particular note are the frescoes by Francesco Solimena (who also did the Heliodorus Driven From the Temple above the door), the works of Luca Giordano, two paintings by de Ribera (extensively restored around 1950) and The Holy Trinity and Saints, perhaps by Guercino (1615). In the great presbytery, closed off by a precious alabaster balustrade and with its vault and walls decorated by beautiful 17th century frescoes, is the main altar, a superb 19th century monument embellished by costly marble and decorations in bronze and semiprecious stones.

3

4

1) Gesù church and square of the same name
2) Gesù church: detail
3) Gesù church: detail of interior
4) The Immacolata spire

Santa Chiara Church and Cloister

Erected between 1310-1328 upon order by Sancia of Mallorca, the wife of Robert of Anjou, the church was built in Gothic-Provençal style. In the middle of the following century it was greatly changed, with heavy baroque remodeling of the interior. Restoration work following the devastating fire in 1943 caused by bombing that nearly completely destroyed it, returned it to its original forms and appearance. Flanked by the imposing bell tower (the lower part of which retained its orig-inal 14th century structure) and preceded by a pronaos with three ogival arches, the center of the façade is adorned with a splendid portal in multicolored marble embellished with elegant inlaid friezes. The interior, with a single rectangular nave flanked by side chapels, holds precious works of art primarily from the 14th-15th centuries. The nine chapels on the left side and those on the right, illuminated by elegant double lancet and three-mullioned windows, hold the tombs of numer-ous noble Neopolitan families, who always favored the Santa Chiara church. One of the most famous tombs in the church is certainly that of Marie of Valois, in the presbytery, with the nearby statue of the no-blewoman and other figures by the great Sienese sculptor Tino di Ca-maino, done around 1339. In the choir behind the altar is the church's most precious jewel, the splendid tomb of Robert I of Anjou. Done between 1343 (the year the king died) and 1345 by the Florentines Giovanni and Pacio Bertini, the work is incomplete due to the collapse of part of the structure. What remains (in particular the sarcophagus of the king resting on pillars flanked by stat-ues of Virtue and depictions of the sovereign and his family) is never-theless sufficient to discern the enormous artistic value that this monument must have had when it was complete. From the choir one enters the large Clarisse cloister, built in the 14th century and remod-eled in 1742, with the addition of a beautiful rustic garden crossed by two avenues, and the marvelous ornamentation in majolica tiles that depict landscapes and rural and mythological scenes.

1) Santa Chiara church: majolica cloister
2) Santa Chiara church: interior

San Domenico Maggiore

1

Preceded by the elaborate San Domenico Spire (1658-1737), the church was erected in Gothic form by order of Charles II of Anjou between 1283 and 1324, on an area previously occupied by a Romanesque church. Starting in the 15th century and until the first half of the 18th century it underwent many changes that obscured its original lines. The later 19th century restoration work produced the same results. The gigantic interior is in the form of a Latin cross with three naves, the two side naves flanked by chapels decorated with frescoes and splendid tombs. Of note on the right is the so-called Capellone del Crocifisso, which holds the 13th century miraculous crucifix that spoke to St. Thomas Aquinas (who lived in the nearby monastery).
In the sacristy, with its vault decorated with an enormous fresco by Francesco Solimena, are the tombs of numerous Aragon princes. The old church, again on the right, houses the oldest known portrait of St. Domenic (early 13th century).

San Severo Chapel

2

At one time the funeral chapel for the Sangro family, the chapel was built in the late 16th century and was later remodeled and embellished in the 17th and 18th centuries. It was originally connected to the nearby Palazzo Sangro by means of a footbridge that was destroyed in 1889. The interior is noteworthy not only for the exquisite tombs it holds, but above all for the frescoes on the vault, done in the mid-18th century by the Neopolitan painter Francesco Maria Russo.
Among the numerous sculptures worthy of note is the splendid Veiled Christ by Giuseppe Sammartino (1753).

1) San Domenico Maggiore church: the façade
2) San Domenico Maggiore church: interior
3) Statue of Nile
4) Santa Maria delle Anime del Purgatorio church: detail

3

4

Piazzetta Nilo

Accessible from the San Severo Chapel by following Via Nilo, this small square and the surrounding district owe their name to a statue of Nile reposing. Dating back to the early centuries of the Roman empire, the group was damaged (the head of Nile has been mutilated) even before the 13th century and then buried. It was not restored until the second half of the 17th century, with the addition of the head of Nile, and placed in its present location. The Sant'Angelo a Nilo church (built in 1358), also known as the Brancaccio chapel for its splendid tomb of Cardinal Rinaldo Brancaccio (to the right of the main altar), its founder, who died in 1423, is located on the square.
Several wellknown contemporary artists contributed to the work, done in Pisa between 1426 and 1428: Donatello (who was also the author of the marvelous bas-relief of the Assumption on the front of the monument), Michelozzo and Pagno di Lapo Portigiani. In addition to other tombs, the chapel's sacristy

contains a beautiful tablet on gold background from the early 16th century depicting Saints Michael and Andrew and precious 15th century wardrobes with inlay decorations.

Via San Biagio dei Librai

From Sant'Angelo a Nilo go down Via San Biagio dei Librai, one of the most characteristic and lively streets in the old city. The street is lined with characteristic shops that display typical handicrafts and items of every sort, often with a characteristic disorder that makes it even more picturesque. Numerous courtly buildings stand along the street, among the most noteworthy of which for its Renaissance architecture is the Palazzo Carafa Santangelo, from the mid-15th century.
A little farther ahead on the right, the enormous Palazzo del Monte di Pietà is famous for the adjoining Pietà Chapel, which 18th century sacristy is one of the high points of 18th century Neopolitan art.

1

2

3

4

1-2-3) San Biagio dei Librai: antiquarian stores
4) View of Via San Biagio dei Librai

TATTOO
VERA PIZZA
TAVOLA CALDA

1 

 2

 3

San Gregorio Armeno

Turning left on San Gregorio Armeno street (famous for its numerous craft shops containing statues of saints and Nativity scene characters, which are often imaginatively placed alongside items from daily and contemporary life), one may see the ancient church of the same name (it was founded before the first half of the 10th century), with the attached monastery, a true jewel of Neapolitan baroque architecture.

1) San Gregorio Armeno
2-3) Nativity scenes and shepherds
4) The Cathedral

4 Cathedral

Built by order of Charles II of Anjou during the late 13th century and opened in 1315 in the presence of Robert of Anjou and his wife Sancia of Mallorca, the cathedral, dedicated to St. Januarius, was built on the site of the earlier Stefania cathedral (from the name of Bishop Stephen I, who founded it in the 5th century), next to the basilica of Santa Restituita, the oldest in the city (4th century). The original Gothic forms were restored and changed numerous times starting in the second half of the 15th century and up to the early 20th century. In particular, the façade is the result of remodeling between the 19th and 20th centuries done on the prior 15th century reconstruction work that had followed the earthquake of 1349. The original structure had three portals, completed in the early 15th century. The most notable of these is the central one, adorned with elegant sculptures by artists that include Tino di Camaino and followers of Nicola Pisano. The grandiose, solemn interior has a Latin cross design divided into three naves with sixteen pillars incorporating over one hundred ancient columns in precious marble on which elegant pointed arches rest. The central nave, with splendid frescoes by Luca Giordano on the walls, is covered by a refined 17th century wooden ceiling adorned with inlay and gilt work, while the side naves are embellished with cross vaults. Under the second arch to the left, the baptismal font is interesting primarily for its basin, on which the 17th century marble and bronze upper portion rests, its basalt surface decorated with curious Bacchic masks. Flanked by statues of St. Paul and St. Peter and closed off by a bronze gate, its right side opens to the large chapel of St. Januarius, built in the first half of the 17th century in homage to the saint who, invoked by the populace, freed the city from the plague in 1527. Here on the back wall are the phials containing the dried blood of the saint, which twice a year, in May and September, liquefy, repeating a miracle with extremely ancient origins that date back to the reign of the Emperor Constantine. On occasion of the miraculous event, considered to bode well for the fate of city, hundreds of Neopolitans gather in the Cathedral to pray to the saint.

Passing the other chapels in the right nave, one enters the transept, which walls continue the series of frescoes on the central nave by Luca Giordano, with a depiction of the Saints. Of note in the third chapel on the right is an Assumption painted by Perugino and his assistants. The Minutolo chapel (the second to the right of the apse), with splendid 13th century mosaic floors in zoomorphic designs, walls decorated with beautiful frescoes from the 14th, 15th and 16th centuries and tombs from the same period, has retained its original 14th century architecture practically unaltered, as has the following Tocco chapel. The apse dates to the 18th century, with vault and walls adorned by frescoes. The entry to the presbytery is flanked by two staircases that lead to the above Carafa, or Succorpo chapel (1497-1506), where the remains of St. Januarius are held in an urn. Passing the lovely chapels on the left of the apse and the transept (one of which contains the tomb of Andrew of Hungary, murdered by order of his wife, Queen Johanna I) and the first three in the left nave, one reaches the Brancaccio chapel, a very elegant 16th century work by the Tuscan Giovanni Antonio Dosio, crowned by an elliptical cupola. Next comes the Santa Restituita chapel, the ancient basilica enclosed in the Cathedral. Inside, where the original Gothic structure is still partially visible despite the remodeling and stucco work later added, Romanera items are preserved along with precious works of art, including the marvelous 14th century mosaic of the Madonna and Child between St. Januarius and St. Restituita by Lello da Orvieto, and two early 13th century marble slabs sculpted with stories of saints. To the far right of the chapel, the baptistery is covered by a cupola bearing remnants of mosaics dating back to the time of its foundation (5th century).

1

2

1) The Archbishop of Naples shows the blood of San Gennaro
2) The baroque San Gennaro spire: the Cathedral in the background

Fourth Part

Piazza Bellini and the ancient Greek walls

Framed by a small green area is the monument to Vincenzo Bellini, erected in 1886 by the Campanian sculptor Alfonso Balzico. The pedestal is adorned by figures (in niches) of the main characters in the great composer's works: La Sonnambula, Norma, Giuletta and Elvira. Nearby are a few remains of the ancient Greek walls: the great blocks of tuff, originally stacked in lines of equal height and width in a so-called isodomum structure, date back to the 4th century B.C., when the primitive settlement of Paleopolis (or Parthenope) was joined by the new agglomerate known as Neapolis.
The nearby theater is also named after Vincenzo Bellini. It was built by the Neopolitan architect Carlo Sorgente during the second half of the 19th century. From Piazza Bellini go along the lively Via Port'Alba, lined with the display windows of numerous book shops, including some of the most famous antiquarian shops in Naples: one of the most interesting, the "Guida" book shop, is a State cultural asset. The street ends at the Port'Alba arch, erected in 1625 but redone in the late 18th century. The door, surmounted by the statue of San Gaetano, stands to the far left of the great hemicycle at Piazza Dante built by Luigi Vanvitelli between 1757 and 1765. The Doric-Roman style work, adorned with statues depicting Virtue, was erected in honor of Charles III.

Piazza Bellini and Greek walls

S. Pietro a Maiella

The church, with 13th-14th century origins, was expanded and extensively remodeled between the late 15th and early 16th centuries, signif-icantly extending the façade beyond the cuspidate bell tower. Further changes were made in its sober architecture until the first half of the 19th century; later work restored its original form. Of the three interior naves, the central one is covered by a splendid ceiling (which continues to the transept), embellished with precious 17th century tapestries depicting episodes in the lives of St. Celestine and St. Catherine of Alexandria. Among these, of most note is certainly that done in 1656-1661 by Mattia Preti, depicting the lives of the two saints. Beautiful tapestries from the 17th and 18th centuries also adorn the chapels in the side naves, while the walls of the transept and apsidal chapels bear precious witness to the original ornamentation: a 14th century wooden Crucifix, frescoes from the same period with Stories of St. Martin and Magdalene, an elegant majolica floor from the 15th century and a 16th century Deposition by Giovanni da Nola.

Croce di Lucca

Next to the San Pietro a Maiella church is the cozy Piazza Luigi Miraglia, which faces the Croce di Lucca church. Erected in the first half of the 17th century, the building was part of the Croce di Lucca convent, where the Polytechnic University now stands.
The interior is remarkable for its beautiful 17th century lacunar ceiling and the colored marble decoration. The Annunciation in the second chapel on the right is attributed to Nicola Malinconico.

Pontano Chapel

To the left on Via dei Tribunali one can visit the Pontano Chapel (1492), one of the greatest expressions of the Neopolitan Renaissance.
The building, with its interior adorned with a marvelous majolica floor with depictions of humans, animals and plants was probably commissioned by the celebrated humanist Giovanni Pontano, at the time the secretary of Ferdinand I of Aragon, in honor of his dead wife and children.

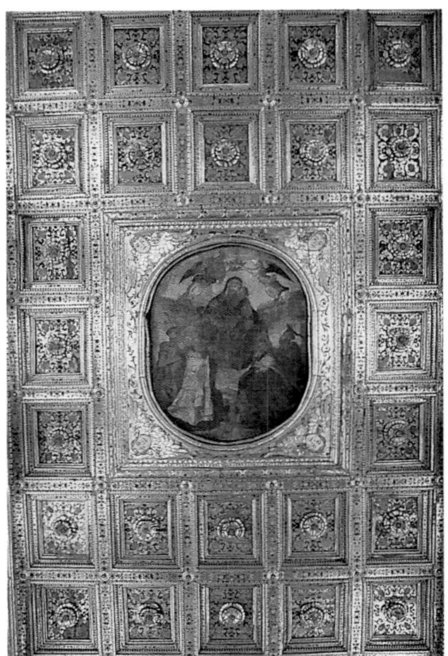

Santa Maria Maggiore

Immediately to the right of the Pontano Chapel, this baroque structure was built between 1653 and 1667, based on a design by Bergamo architect Cosimo Fanzago. The gracious cuspidate Romanesque bell tower, which dates back to the 11th-12th century, belonged to a previously existing basilica erected during the first half of the 6th century, where the present church is now located.

1-2) Croce di Lucca church
3) Pontano chapel

1

2

3

San Giovanni a Carbonara

From Via dei Tribunali, turning left onto Via Duomo and passing the Santa Maria Donnaregina church (perhaps the most noteworthy Gothic church in the city, with its splendid frescoes and 14th century tombs, which include that of Queen Maria of Hungary in the apse, by Tino di Camaino), one enters Via Settembrini. Going on toward the right is Via San Giovanni a Carbonara, at the end of which a majestic stairway leads to the church of the same name. Like the nearby convent, its construction work continued for 50 years, from the mid-14th to the early 15th century. The beautiful 15th century portal open on the right side gives access to the single, rectangular nave within, which contains some of the most precious sculptures in Naples. The splendid tomb of King Ladislas, brother of Johanna II, supported by four gigantic Virtues and adorned by statues (by Marco and Andrea da Firenze) and painted figures (by Leonardo da Besozzo); the unfinished tomb of Ser Gianni Caracciolo dates from the same period, embellished with an inscription by Lorenzo Valla and sculptures by Andrea da Firenze. Another very interesting monument is that by the Miroballos, completed in the 16th century and rich with precious sculptures.

Santa Caterina a Formiello

Going back down Via San Giovanni a Carbonara and heading toward the train station, one reaches the Piazza Enrico De Nicola, where directly to the left of the Porta Capuana is the splendid church of Santa Caterina a Formiello, built in the 16th century (perhaps based on a design by Francesco di Giorgio Martini), in beautiful Renaissance form. The Latin cross interior contains excellent 18th century paintings by Paolo de Matteis as well as numerous works dating from the foundation of the church or early in the next century.

1) Santa Maria Maggiore church: interior
2) San Giovanni a Carbonara church
3) Santa Caterina a Formiello church

Fifth Part

National Archeological Museum

Located in a large building dating back to the late 16th century, the museum grew around collections of the Farnese family, bequeathed to Charles Bourbon by his mother Elisabetta Farnese. Enlarged over the course of the years with discoveries from Herculaneum, Pompeii, Cumae and other excavation sites, the Borgia collection of precious Egyptian objects as well as numerous purchases, acquisitions and donations, the museum has one of the largest and most important collections of classical antiquities in the world. Its works are priceless, including sculptures, paintings, mosaics (nearly all of which, like the frescoes, come from Herculaneum and Pompeii) furnishings from the Villa dei Papiri in Herculaneum, terracottas and ivories, jewels and bronzes, prehistoric findings and ancient coins from the Santangelo collection. Its collection is so vast that only the most familiar works can be mentioned here, leaving it up to the visitor to discover most of the museum's treasures. For example, the marble sculptures include masterpieces such as The Aristogeiton and Harmodius Tyrannicides, a Roman copy of an original bronze from the 4th century B.C., the majestic Athena Farnese, a copy from the Imperial Rome era of a Greek original, perhaps by Phidias; the moving marble relief of Orpheus and Eurydice with the god Hermes; the splendid copy of the celebrated Doryphorus by Polyclitus, found in Pompeii in the late 18th century; the harmonious Ephebe Carrying the Lamp, a reproduction of an original done in the 4th century B.C., also found in Pompeii on Via dell'Abbondanza (1925); The Dead Amazon, one of the copies of celebratory groups commissioned by King Attalus of Pergamon in the 2nd century B.C.; the seductive Venus Callipige, a Roman copy of a Greek original that adorned the Domus Auria of Nero in Rome; the decapitated Venus di Snuessa; the mighty Farnese Hercules, a copy of an original bronze from Lisippo; and the exceptionally dynamic Farnese Bull group (the largest that has survived from ancient times), completed in the 2nd-3rd century B.C. based on an original Greek bronze. In the collection of mosaics, nearly all from Pompeii, the most famous is certainly the enormous Battle of Alexander against Darius, done in Alexandria, Egypt, which adorned the floor of one of the rooms in the House of the Faun in Pompeii, where it was discovered in 1831.

1

2

3

1) Archeological Museum: the façade
2) The Farnese Hercules
3) The Farnese Eros
4) Spring: fresco

4

1

1) The Farnese Bull

2) Portrait of a young girl

2

2

3

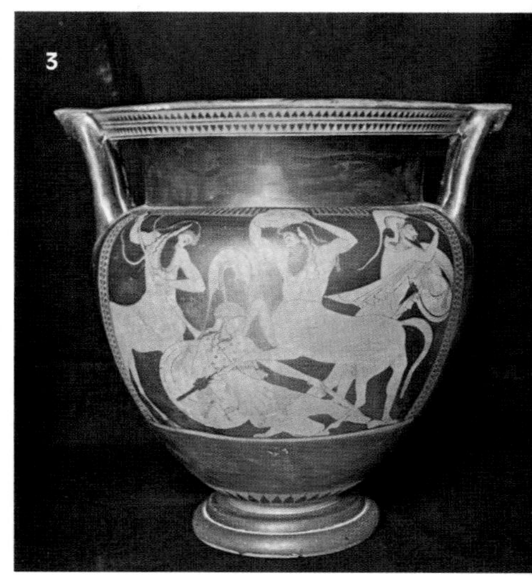

4

5

1) Perseus and Andromeda
2) Drunken Silenus
3) Crater of Myson
4) Hydria Vivenzio
5) Gold and silver jewelry found in the excavations of Herculaneum and Pompei

1

2

1) The rustic concert
2) Bathing Aphrodite and her maidens

1

1

The Catacombs

Excavated at Capodimonte in the yellow tuff of the Aminei hills, they are built on two underground levels, with wide tunnels adorned with precious paintings and excellent mosaics from the 3rd to 10th centuries. The original nucleus of the catacombs was a nobleman's tomb from the late 2nd century (today the lower vestibule), donated to the primitive Christian community of the city. Decorated with simple geometrical, floral and zoomorphic motifs, around the 4th century it was joined by a catacomb basilica, noteworthy for the isolated altar and the bishop's throne excavated in the tuffaceous wall.
In the 5th century the remains of the martyr St. Januarius, decapitated in Pozzuoli in 305, were moved here, and from this point on the catacombs assumed their present name and were significantly expanded, starting from the two original vestibules with long tunnels traced by arcosolia, cubicula, and superimposed niches.

2

1) San Gennaro catacombs
2) Precious mosaic found in the San Gennaro catacombs

1

2

Capodimonte Museum and National Galleries

The collections are located in the Palazzo Reale di Capodimonte, commissioned by Charles Bourbon in 1738. Immersed in a large wooded park with extensive English gardens, the majestic edifice was not completed until 1838, and in the first half of the 20th century was remodeled so that it could adequately house its priceless collection. In addition to the National Gallery and various minor collections, the institution includes the 19th Century Gallery, the Historical Apartment, the porcelain and ceramic Collections, the Armory and the Porcelain Room.
The National Gallery developed around an original core of masterpieces belonging to the Farnese family bequeathed to Charles Bourbon in 1731, and was subsequently enlarged with numerous other

1-2) Capodimonte Royal Palace and park. The site of the Capodimonte Museum and Galleries

1

2

3

works and collections acquired, donated or taken from churches, until it assumed its current vast proportions. The collection of paintings is especially rich, starting with the seven precious tapestries depicting episodes of the battle of Pavia, based on cartoons done by Bernart van Orley in the Brussels workshop in 1525-1531. There are thousands of masterpieces in the galleries; it is impossible to mention them all. They include the majestic altarpiece by Simone Martini with St. Ludwig of Toulouse, painted in 1317 by the Sienese painter to celebrate the coronation of Robert of Anjou as king of Naples, the Crucifixion painted by Masaccio in 1426-1427, part of a valuable polyptych which was broken up, a Renaissance Madonna with Child and Angels by Botticelli and the celebrated portrait of Luca Pacioli done by an anonymous artist in 1495. In the rooms containing 15th and 16th century paintings, of note is the Holy Family with San Giovannino and two portraits of Clement VII by the Venetian Sebastiano del Piombo, while the Emilian Correggio is represented by numerous works, including the famous Gypsy Girl. After the Lucrezia by Parmigianino, the amazing Transfiguration by Giovanni Bellini di-

4

1) Ceramic: the Goose dishware set
2) The Goose dishware set: detail
3) Detail of the Ball Room
4) Flower box of the 18th century
5) Giovanni Bellini: Transfiguration
6) Gigante: Amalfi coast

5

6

1

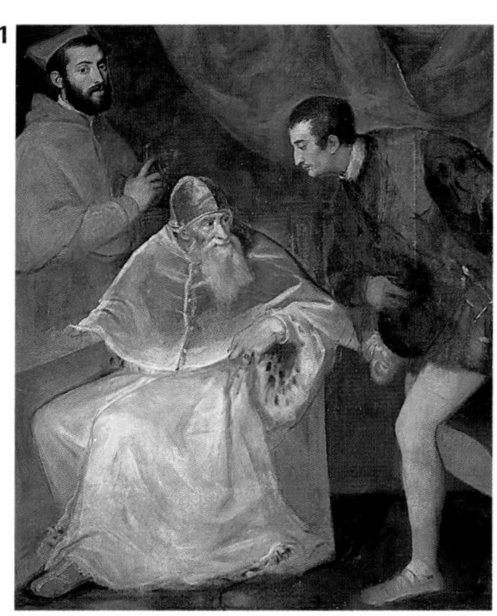

2

3

4

5

vides the hall, with masterpieces by Lorenzo Lotto, Palma Vecchio, El Greco and other masters. There are three portraits of Pope Paul II by Titian, who was favored by the Farnese family, as well as one of Cardinal Alessandro Farnese (1543) and a delicate Danae (1545). Of the Flemish painters, next to Pieter Brueghel's The Blind Leading the Blind (1568) there is also Joos van Cleve. As testimony to the pricelessness of the works in the other halls, suffice it to list the most famous masters with works displayed: Raphael, Michelangelo, Caravaggio, Rembrandt, Gido Reni, Luca Giordano and great Neopolitan painters like Gaspare Traversi. The extremely rich 19th Century Gallery offers an unusually broad panorama of Italian

6

(with particular attention to Neopolitan works) and foreign painting of the period, while the porcelain and ceramic collection, containing three thousand pieces, demonstrates the pomp and elegance of the noble residences (and eating halls) of the 18th and 19th centuries. This is also beautifully represented by the enchanting Queen Maria Amalia's Room, entirely decorated in rococo style and containing over three thousand pieces of the finest porcelain.

7

8

1) Titian: Paolo Farnese II with grandchildren
2) Letizia Bonaparte, by Canova
3) Bourbon Arms Room: horseman and horse armor
4) Luca Giordano: St. Francis Xavier baptizes the grandchildren and St. Francesco Borgia
5-6) Arms Hall
7) Ball Room
8) Ceramic: equestrian group from the Goose collection

2

3

Sixth Part

Vomero

Following Via Salvator Rosa from the Archeological Museum, the first building on the left is the Gesù e Maria Hospital (with the attached church of the same name, founded in the 16th century), then the Piazza Mazzini, and nearby, the 17th century Santa Maria della Pazienza church. Continuing along Via della Cerra and Via San Gennaro ad Antignano, turn left at the Piazza degli Artisti onto Via Luca Giordano and then left again onto Via Alessandro Scarlatti, the whole length of which crosses Vomero. This area, which developed in the late 19th century as a residential district for the Neopolitan bourgeoisie, underwent profound changes during the fifties and sixties, turning it into one of the most disorganized and congested areas of the city. The elegant homes of the belle époque were gradually replaced by gigantic apartment buildings one on top of the other, but the vertiginous growth in population in the area was not matched by adequate urbanization, especially with respect to the road system (despite the opening of new roads at its periphery), with the resulting increased problems caused primarily by heavy traffic. Connected to the lower quarters of the city by three cable car lines, the district nevertheless preserves some of the city's principal monuments: the Castel Sant'Elmo, the S. Martino Carthusian monastery and the Villa Floridiana, surrounded by a marvelous park.

Villa Floridiana

The villa, near the Chiaia cable car station that connects Vomero with Corso Vittorio Emanuele below, owes its name to Lucia Migliaccio Partanna, the Duchess of Floridia, in honor of whom it was built between 1817 and 1819. Ferdinand I of Bourbon, who in 1814 had wed the

1) Masaccio: Crucifixion
2) The Floridiana Museum
3) The park of Villa Floridiana

1

2

3

Duchess in a second marriage, made the decision to erect the splendid residence on grounds of expediency. As her marriage to the sovereign was morganatic, she had not received the title of queen and thus could not reside at the royal palace of the Bourbons. Following protocol, Ferdinand I then bought the vast tract of land on the hill of Vomero, where a luxurious villa was already located, in order to create a summer residence for the duchess. The Tuscan architect Antonio Niccolini, who had also made the changes in the Palazzo Partanna on the Piazza dei Martiri, another residence which Ferdinand gave to his second wife, was in charge of the expansion and remodeling work. Particular care was taken in developing the large park, gently descending toward the sea along the slopes of the hill. Dominated by trees such as holm oaks, plane trees and cedars, the park alternates in carefully planned and very scenic sequences of open lawns and shady woods, English garden areas adorned by the splendid springtime flowering of camellias, and steep slopes, wide avenues, showy esplanades and little paths with panoramic views (one can see the whole city, the gulf and even the nearby isle of Capri from here). There are little temples and folies, those picturesque imitations of ruins that are also known as capricci, so often used in English-style parks.

The main building, which appears in all its beauty against the background of a large lawn at the end of the main avenue (partially modified from Niccolini's design in the late 19th

4

5

century), is an elegant residence in neoclassical style, which architecture recalls the sumptuous villas of Pompeii. Damaged during the Second World War, the building, currently owned by the State, was carefully restored so that it might better serve as the Duca di Martina National Ceramic Museum, one of the largest collections entirely dedicated to the decorative arts, which it has housed since 1927. The original collection was the result of the collecting passion of Placido de Sangro, Duke of Martina, who during the second half of the 19th century gathered numerous examples of Italian, European and Oriental porcelain and majolica, as well as items in glass, coral, ivory and other materials traditionally used in the minor decorative arts, which were quite fashionable at the time. His nephew the Count de Marzi added to the collection, which was then donated to the State in the early 20th century. The museum was further enriched in 1978 when Riccardo de Sangro, the heir of the Duke of Martina family, bequeathed the museum a large collection (over 500 pieces) of other porcelain and majolica acquired by his ancestor in the 19th century, along with valuable furnishings.

6

The visit begins on the ground floor of the villa, which opens to the large atrium in which the portraits of Ferdinand I of Bourbon, done by an anonymous 19th century painter, and of the Duchess of Floridia, probably by Vincenzo Camuccini, are displayed. The rooms contain collections of majolica which include splendid Spanish-Moorish pieces from Malaga and Valencia, Italian ceramics from the 16th century with most refined ornamentation, produced by artisans from Deruta, Gubbio, Faenza, Urbino, Cafaggiolo and Palermo, and precious 17th century examples of Venetian and Abruzzo works. The same floor contains Italian, Arabian and Byzantine wooden jewel boxes and cases, inlaid or studded with semiprecious stones, silver and ivory frames, Murano glass and Bohemian crystals, with pieces from the 15th to the 18th centuries, Italian and European medieval ivory and enamel work and precious snuffboxes. On the first floor, preceded by an anteroom with a portrait of the Duke of Martina, are the rooms which display the prestigious collection of porcelain, mostly 18th century, where in addition to the rich collection of Meissen china there are equally precious items produced in Capodimonte, Venice, Naples, Chantilly, Sèvres and Vincennes, as well as German china from Berlin, Niderviller and Frankenthal, and from Vienna, Zurich, and the Wedgwood and Chelsea factories. This quite vast production of hard and soft paste porcelain includes table settings, walking sticks with porcelain handles, and frames, medallions and vases. Of great interest is also the collection of Oriental art, one of the largest collections in Italy, containing over 1000 porcelain pieces from Japan and China. Split up between the basement floor of the Villa and the first floor, it includes some most valuable pieces of refined white and blue Chinese porcelain in the "green family" and the "pink family," a precious Chinese vase from the "black family," pieces from the Ming dynasty, ivory, lacquer work and small Chinese and Indian bronzes.

7

1) Cage-shaped clock
2) Vase depicting the adoration of the Magi
3) Cabaret: German porcelain
4) 18th century goblet and candelabra
5) The china made by the Real Fabbrica of Naples
6) Ceramics from the 18th century
7) Folding fan

1

Castel Sant'Elmo

2

Robert of Anjou ordered the construction of this castle in 1329. The Sienese Tino di Camaino, who was building the nearby San Martino Carthusian monastery at the same time, contributed to the initial part of its construction. Completed over 20 years later, the mighty structure was then redone in the first half of the 17th century by order of the viceroy Pedro of Toledo. The austere construction, partially dug into the tuffaceous rock of Vomero and with a star-shaped design, has no towers (originally substituted by gigantic cannons located on the corners of the structure), but has a deep moat that surrounds it on three sides and a number of blockhouses built at various times.
It became quite strategically important over the centuries, becoming a theater for crucial events in the history of the city, starting from the assault of the troops of Johanna I in 1348 until the Masaniello revolt three centuries later.

1) Sant'Erasmo Church, seen from the glacises of Castel Sant'Elmo
2) View of Castel Sant'Elmo

San Martino Carthusian Monastery

This was built between 1325 and 1368 by order of Charles of Anjou. The church, opened in 1368 but greatly modified in the late 16th century, is a splendid example of Neopolitan baroque architecture. Inside, it has a single nave, with side chapels replacing the original naves on the right and left in the 16th century. Even the splendid marble ornamentation, done between the late 16th and early 17th centuries based on a design by the Tuscan Giovanni Antonio Dosio, was retouched several times in 18th century work that further embellished it. The most famous painting in the church, the large Deposition (1838) by Massimo Stanzione (who has numerous other works in the church), is located at the portal. Nevertheless, The Twelve Prophets by Spagnoletto from the first half of the 17th century, located in the chapel arches, is equally precious. Among the numerous artists who worked on the very rich painted ornamentation of the church are Guido Reni (author of the incomplete Nativity on the back wall of the presbytery), Battista Caracciolo (of particular note are the beautiful frescoes with the Story of Mary in the vault of the third chapel on the left and The Washing of the Feet on the left wall of the presbytery), Luca Giordano (who did the Triumph of Judith on the ceiling of the Tesoro chapel), Carlo Maratta and Francesco Solimena. From the church, through the adjoining Procuratori cloister, one enters the splendid gardens of the monastery, which offer spectacular views.

1

2

3

1-2) San Martino Carthusian monastery: the cloister
3) Glimpse of large cloister
4) San Martino Carthusian monastery: detail of the court

4

San Martino National Museum

With its various sections, the picture gallery and the sculpture collection, the museum is located in the San Martino Carthusian monastery.
From the first section, the Naval display, where models of boats and ships from the 17th to 19th centuries are displayed, go on to the section that contains historical memories of the Reign of Naples, the first room of which includes the celebrated Tavola Strozzi, done in the mid-15th century and most recently attributed to Francesco Rosselli. The plate, painted in temperas, depicts the triumphal reentry of the Spanish fleet of Ferrante of Aragon after the battle of Ischia in 1465 against the Anjevins. The realistic depiction of the city as it must have appeared in the 15th century, painted in the background, is a precious testimony for the study of ancient topography and the urban development of Naples. In the halls, there are various items (coffers, ceramics, prints, medallions, objects belonging to famous persons, vases, arms and more) as well as portraits of illustrious persons and royalty in Neopolitan history (numerous Bourbon princes, including an excellent copy of Charles III of Bourbon by Goya, a portrait of Admiral Nelson, various works depicting Joachim Murat, including The Marriage of Murat and Caroline Bonaparte), and paintings depicting important episodes in the history of Naples (The Masaniello Revolt, The Battle of Leipzig, The Taking of the City by John of Austria, The Opening of the Naples-Portici Railway, Garibaldi at Volturno) and beautiful Neopolitan landscapes. In the last room in this section one may go to the lookout and enjoy a most spectacular and evocative view of Naples and its gulf, or else go to the section devoted to Neopolitan Topography. Here are displayed precious old maps of the city, including the exceptional map done in 1566 by the Frenchman Antonio Lafréry, as well as paintings from various periods depicting views of the city and other areas of Campania. Some of the rooms that originally were the apartment of the prior of the monastery, with enormous frescoes from the 18th century on the vaults, contain the Festivals and Customs section, where the antique clothing and costumes are a backdrop to a series of gracious 18th century watercolors

1

2

1) 13th century sculpture: The Cardinal Virtues
2) Tavola Strozzi: The port of Naples
3) Domenico Gargiulo: Masaniello Revolt

3

depicting Pulcinella, the famous mask of the city, and paintings from the 18th and 19th centuries dedicated to the traditional festivals (Carnival of 1711, Feast of the Madonna dell'Arco, Fiera di San Germano). Of particular note are the rooms containing the Nativity scene sections, in which lovely little statues and antique Nativity scenes are displayed, primarily from the 18th century. This traditional art so dear to Naples, in which numerous artists and craftsmen have participated over the centuries, produced the two rarest pieces in the collection: the Cuciniello Nativity scene, with over 200 finely crafted persons and animals, and the Ricciardi Nativity scene, enlivened by about a hundred meticulously carved and painted figurines. The 19th century miniature Nativity scene in an eggshell is curious and is probably the smallest in the world. Some rooms in this section are devoted to Neopolitan theater: they include interesting paintings which depict the Teatro San Carlo before the fire of 1816 that completely destroyed the hall and other parts of the building. To reach the Picture Gallery one crosses the large monastery cloister, a wide green area surrounded by a splendid arcade designed by Giovanni Antonio Dosio in the late 16th century. The cloister structure was partially modified in the next century by Cosimo Fanzago of Bergamo, who is responsible for much of the elegant decoration and the small cemetery fence. The large collection of paintings in the rooms include various subjects from different periods, from an Epiphany by the Greeks Angelo and Donato Bizamano (16th century) and a 17th century Marina by Salvator Rosa, the

1 

Portrait of the Sabine Women by Luca Giordano and the Parts of the World by Ribera (with a painting by Giordano depicting the same subject displayed in the same room), to an awesome Landscape by Alessandro Magnasco, a splendid Self-Portrait by Francesco Solimena and the still lifes and paintings of animals and flowers by the Neopolitans Tommaso Realfonso and Baldassarre De Caro and the Flemish Brueghel. Two entire rooms are devoted to Neopolitan painters of the second half of the 19th century (including Domenico Morelli and Vincenzo Gemito), followed by the last rooms, with portraits and landscapes (Portrait of the Architect Chelli by Gaetano Forte; Portrait by Filippo Palizzi; Landscape by Giuseppe Palizzi; Winter Sunset by Federico Rossano; The Country Curate by Marco De Gregorio).
The sculpture section includes many interesting works that cover a vast period of time: from the 1st century A.D. there is a Roman sepulcher reused as a tomb centuries later, while from the 14th century there are precious sculptures by Tino di Camaino, who was quite active in Naples during the first half of the 14th century. The splendid objects displayed in the Minor Arts Rooms include a glass collection (with very refined 15th century examples of Murano production and 16th century items from both Italian and foreign workshops), mirrors, 18th century porcelain from the Real Fabbrica of Naples and from Sèvres, and jewels. Of particular note are the 16th century antiphonaries, illuminated with surprising perfection.

2

3

1) Jacob Philippe Hackert: Launch of the Partenope at Castellammare
2) 13th century sculpture
3) St. Martin National Museum: Prince of St. Antimo, Vincenzo Rufolo with his children. Signed by Eduardo Dubrefé and dated 1851

1

2

1) Candido Francesco Saverio: Portrait of Cimarosa
2) Ter Bruggren: Portrait thought to be of Masaniello
3) Salvatore Fergola: Opening of the Naples-Portici Railway

Page 77
1) Corso Umberto I and Piazza Borsa
2) Del Carmine church

3

1

2

Seventh Part

Piazza Municipio and Corso Umberto I

From the Piazza Municipio, Via Depretis proceeds to the Piazza Giovanni Bovio, with a fountain of Neptune at its center and faced by the Palazzo della Borsa. Built in the late 19th century, the building contains the Sant'Aspreno al Porto chapel, which was founded in the 8th century. The piazza marks the beginning of Corso Umberto I, a wide road opened in the last decade of the 19th century and known as "Il Rettifilo" for its straightness.

Santa Maria del Carmine

Not far from the Piazza del Mercato is the Piazza del Carmine, on which left side stands the basilica of Santa Maria del Carmine. Very old (perhaps the 12th century), it was expanded and remodeled by the early 14th century at the order of Elizabeth of Bavaria, the mother of Conradin of Swabia, who was buried with Frederick of Baden, Duke of Austria, his cousin and companion in adventure, who were both decapitated in October 1268 on the Piazza del Mercato by order of Charles of Anjou. Other changes (including the façade) were made between the 17th and 18th centuries. The right side of the church is flanked by a tall, imposing 15th century bell tower culminating in a majolica cusp added in the first half of the 17th century: the arch that opens to the center gives access to the convent cloister attached to the basilica, with the vault and walls of its arcade decorated with 16th-17th century frescoes. The interior of the basilica, with a single nave flanked by chapels, is beautifully decorated with multicolored marble added by 17th and 18th century artists. Of interest in the first chapel on the right is the pulpit located where Masaniello gave his speech to the crowd just before being betrayed and killed in the convent. The Carmine basilica holds the tomb of the popular hero, although its exact location was kept hidden and is still unknown. The same chapel holds a precious tapestry by

Mattia Preti depicting the Virgin and St. Simon. At the transept arch there is a 14th century wooden crucifix which was considered miraculous until the 15th century. Another wooden crucifix, this one from the 15th century, is preserved in the chapel to the left of the transept, embellished by a Crucifixion which may be by Francesco Solimena. The choir contains a small plate depicting the Madonna della Bruna, done in the 14th century: the icon, greatly venerated by the people, was originally located in the small church that stood in the area currently occupied by the basilica.

Piazza Garibaldi

From the Santa Maria del Carmine church after Piazza Pepe, go down Corso Garibaldi, which proceeds straight until it widens into the Piazza Nolana not far from the Circumvesuviana station. Here, to the right, is the Gate of the same name, flanked by two towers representing Faith and Hope. On the arch of the gate, built into the city walls in the 15th century and still miraculously standing despite centuries of stormy history, especially the violent bombings in this part of the city, one may note the bas-relief from the same period depicting Ferdinand I of Aragon. Proceeding along Corso Garibaldi, one comes to the Piazza Garibaldi. Built in our century, the very large square is decorated with a monument to the Hero of the Two Worlds by the Florentine sculptor Cesare Zocchi in 1904. In front of the square is the main train station, built between 1959 and 1970.

Piazza Ferrovia

Surrounding Areas

Mt. Vesuvius

According to geologists, the origins of the only active volcano on continental Europe and the undisputed symbol of Naples and the entire Campania region go back about 12,000 years, when seismic activity under the earth's crust transformed a previous volcano into what would much later become Vesuvius.
After a period of early eruptions, starting around the 8th century B.C. the volcano went into a long period of inactivity; at that time it must have been about 2000 meters high, much higher than its present 1270 meters. In addition, its slopes, which are now mostly barren, must have been covered with the dense vegetation typical of Mediterranean scrub. The beginnings of Mt. Vesuvius' historical activity, culminating in the catastrophic eruption of 79 A.D. that buried Pompeii and

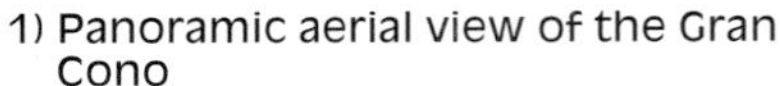

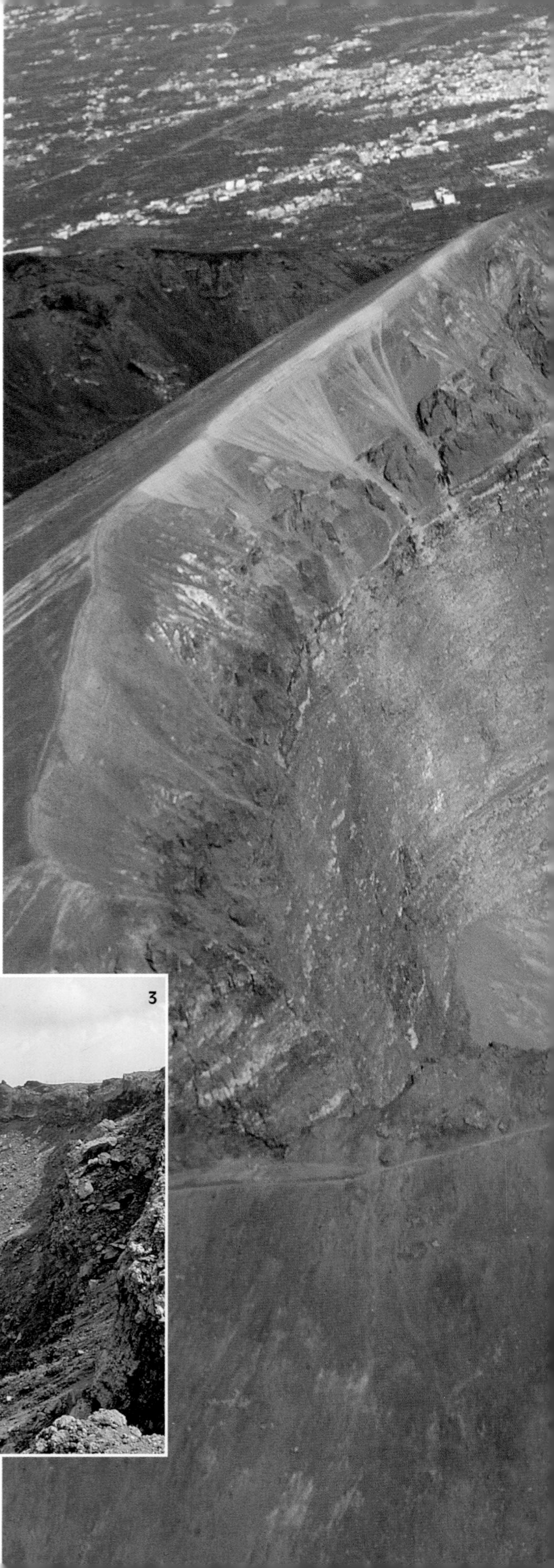

1) Panoramic aerial view of the Gran Cono
2-3) Lava formations

1

2

3

4

5

Herculaneum, may be traced to 63 A.D., when the entire Campania region was shaken by a devastating earthquake. Sixteen years later, the tremendous eruption later described by Pliny the Younger was again preceded by strong earthquakes, which were almost immediately followed by a devastating explosion. The uncontainable pressure of the incandescent magma and gases opened up an underground conduit and spewed out with awesome violence in the form of boiling mud, lava, rocks, lapilli, poisonous gases and ashes, ripping apart one side of

6

7

1) Detail which shows the modifying action of the lava flows on the area
2) Detail of a typical "ropy"lava formation
3) Effusive phase
4-5) Views of the route running from the Colle to the crater
6) Evocative image of the snow covered crater
7) Active fumaroles

the mountain and bringing death and destruction all around it. Scientists believe that Vesuvius assumed its present appearance on that occasion. Other less violent eruptions occurred until the 16th century, when the volcano seemed to have become inactive. However, it once again violently exploded in 1631, causing thousands of deaths and inestimable damage. These alternating phases of calm and volcanic activity continued until the early 20th century, when in 1906 the volcano exploded again, once more changing part of its morphology. The last destructive eruption was in 1944, when the summit formed a large crater completely covered with yellow ash.

1) Panoramic view of the route leading to the crater
2-4) Two moments during the climbing to the crater

3) Detail of the path making it possible to descend into the interior of the crater

1

2

3

4

Herculaneum

Herculaneum, founded by Hercules according to mythological tradition, actually did have Greek origins, as demonstrated by the few remaining traces of the most ancient city walls and the layout of the town, with cardines and decumani built at right angles. The Greeks of Neapolis and Cumae ruled Herculaneum as from the 6th century B.C., while in the 5th century the Samnites gained control, and the town remained under their domination for centuries.
Between the 2nd and 1st centuries B.C., Herculaneum took part in the "Allies' War" against Rome, but in 89 B.C. it was conquered and transformed into a municipium. After the conquest it developed in demographic, political and urban terms. Its economy was not based on commerce and crafts; Herculaneum was a highclass resort with many patrician residences and few buildings destined for business activities, where life must have jogged on at a fairly relaxed pace.
In 63 A.D. the town was hit by the earthquake which devastated all of Campania. It had not yet recovered from that catastrophe when, on

1) Panorama
2) Mosaic of the Triclinio

2

1

1

2

3

4

24th August in the year 79 A.D., it was engulfed by a huge river of boiling mud and debris produced by the terrifying eruption of Vesuvius, which totally inundated it. The population probably had time to attempt an escape towards the sea, but they were forced back to the shore by a violent tidal wave, as witnessed by the human remains and remains of boats recently found along the coast. When the eruption ended, Herculaneum was covered with a thick layer of mud (at some points over 10 metres deep); abandoned by its inhabitants, the town was never rebuilt, and only later did the town of Resina grow up at the edges of and partly on the area where

1) Panorama
2) "Trellis" house
3) Decumano Massimo
4) House of the Relief of Tefelo

1

Herculaneum once stood. The very mud that sealed its fate has preserved the town to the present day. As it dried and solidified, it turned into a kind of thick, compact blanket which adhered to every structure and household article, thus protecting everything which escaped the river of mud and debris, and preserving (among other things) the upper floors of the buildings. Although numerous masonry structures were damaged by the shock wave, entire rooms have been brought to light practically intact. The layer of mud also preserved wood, a material which normally soon deteriorates unless suitably protected. The first discovery of remains of the ancient city was as recent as 1709, when the Austrian Prince d'Elboeuf discovered part of the Theatre by chance. Further research, conducted as from 1738 in accordance with the tunnel and shaft system, brought to light among other things the "Villa of Scrolls", situated near the town, which is celebrated for its collection of sculptures and a library consisting of around 2000 papyrus scrolls. The excavations were closed in 1766; they only recommenced in 1828, this time using the more modern method of open-air excavation, and continued until 1855. In 1869 work began again, but the results were very disappointing, and excavation was interrupted in 1875. Amedeo Maiuri recommenced the research with scientific rigour in 1927, and it has continued until the present day.

2

1) "Cardo V"
2) A shop
3) View over the Gym

Page 92-93. Herculaneum: digs

3

Pompeii

Located on the slopes of Mt. Vesuvius, this ancient city probably grew up around an Oscan Campanian settlement founded around 600 B.C., which due to its fortunate geographical position developed rapidly. First subjugated by the Etruscans, then the Cumaeans, it finally became a Roman colony in 89 B.C. This total loss of autonomy nevertheless ushered in a great flowering of the city that affected all facets of its economic, architectural and artistic life.
This period of prosperity and splendor was brusquely interrupted in 63 A.D. by the violent earthquake that devastated the entire Campania region and inflicted severe damage on Pompeii. The city nevertheless recovered from the catastrophe and almost immediately began the rebuilding (especially of private buildings) necessary to regain the prosperity that had marked it in the past. But on August 24 of 79 A.D. the awesome eruption of Vesuvius put a final end to its good fortune. Pompeii, which by a tragic irony of

1) The Forum: detail
2) Aerial view of the arc haelogical digs
3) The Amphitheater

1

2

1

2

3

fate had developed on land originating from a river of lava which had erupted from the volcano centuries before, was hit by a giant cloud of poisonous gases, ash, lapilli and incandescent rocks that buried monuments and humans under a curtain of detritus more than 7 meters deep. Literally erased by the devastating fury of the volcano, the city remained buried until 1748, when the first excavations were begun. Still under way, archaeological research has discovered over 60 hectares of the land on which the city must have existed at the time of the catastrophe.
Entirely walled, Pompeii was a populous and much visited city with numerous hotels, inns, post-stages (concentrated near the city gates), shops (some of which still bear their decorated signs), private homes (from the oldest and simplest of the 4th century B.C. to the luxurious, sumptuously decorated ones of the 1st century A.D.), and large public monuments (temples, the basilica,

4

1) Mill and oven
2) Cast of body found in a garden
3) House of Lucrezio Frontone: detail
4) House of the Tragic Poet: entrance mosaic - detail
5) The Basilica
6) Foro Civile: western ambulacrum

5

6

1

2

3

1) Villa of the Mysteries: Room of the Large Painting
2) Villa of the Mysteries: The terrified woman
3) Villa of the Mysteries: The whipped girl and the naked Bacchante
4) House of the Vettii: perystilium - detail

4 ▸▸

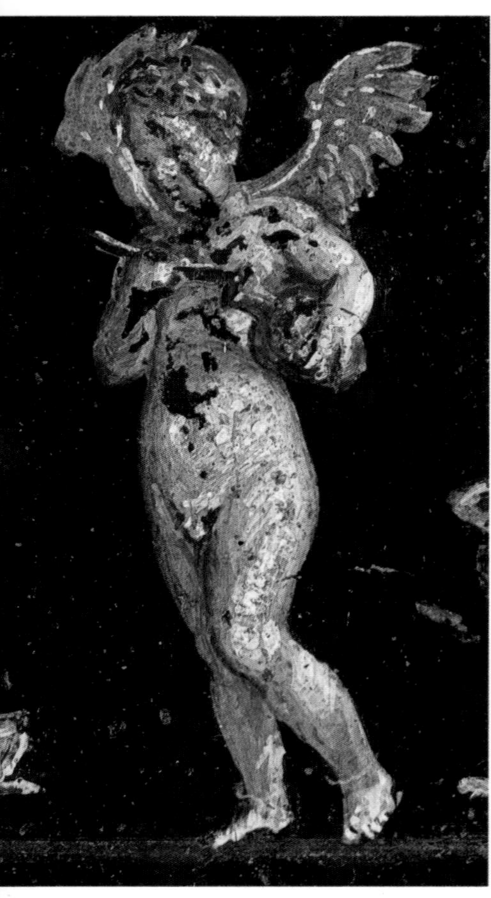

thermal baths, the covered market, theaters and the Forum buildings). The thousands of finds contained in the National Archeological Museum in Naples bear witness to the opulence and elegance of the city: mosaics, sculptures and precious objects from the courtly Pompeian residences, rechristened with evocative names (House of the Faun, of the Gilt Cupids, of the Ephebe, of the Labyrinth, and the Villa of Mysteries at the edge of the city), which in many cases still preserve ornamentation which is surprisingly magnificent and elegant and has lost none of its original charm.

1) House of the Vettii: detail of a fresco
2) House of the Vettii: Apollo conquering the Python
3) House of the Vettii: Priapus weighing his phallus

3

Capri

Celebrated the world over for its extraordinary natural beauty, for the Blue Grotto, the Faraglioni, the Natural Arch, and its picturesque reefs with fanciful names, their peaks often dominated by ancient watch towers, the hollows of crystalline water, the spectacular views and the mundane liveliness of the famous Piazzetta, the island, almost entirely formed of calcareous rock, is quite rich with splendid monuments. Among the most ancient are the imposing remains of the Baths of Tiberius and the two splendid imperial residences, Villa Damecuta and Villa Jovis. Capri town contains

1 

2 

3 

4

the 17th century Santo Stefano cathedral, the vast San Giacomo Carthusian monastery, built in the 14th century, and the spectacular Via Krupp. In Anacapri, immersed in the quiet of vineyards and olive groves and connected to the Marina Grande by the ancient Phoenician Stairs, is the splendid Villa San Michele, where the Swedish physician and writer Axel Munthe amassed countless ancient finds.

1) The spectacular Via Krupp
2) Villa San Michele: view of the Loggia
3) A beautiful view of the funicular railway
4) The Marina Grande seen from Villa San Michele
5) The magnificent architectural complex of the San Giacomo Charterhouse among olive trees and vineyards
6) The "Faraglioni" (The Stacks)

5

6

1

1) Panoramic view of the Piazzetta
2) Villa San Michele: a glimpse of the Loggia with Hermes at rest in the foreground
3) Curtius Malaparte's highly original villa at the top of Punta Masullo
4) View of the Faraglioni at night
5) The unforgettable panorama to be enjoyed from Monte Solaro
6) The lights, colours and magic of the fascinating Grotta Azzurra

2

3

4

5

6

1

1) Marina Grande: the port
2) Bathing establishment and the port of Marina Grande
3) Villa Jovis: the ruins of the grand villa
4) Anacapri: the lighthouse
5) Plan of Villa Jovis
6) The chair lift that leads from Anacapri to Monte Solaro
7) Aerial view of Capri island

2

3

4

5

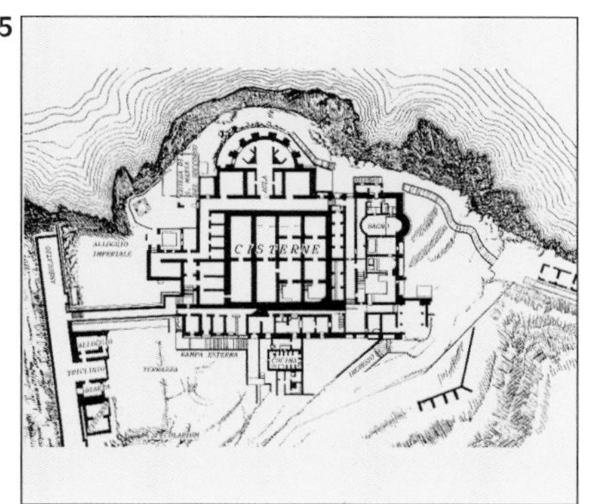
CISTERNE
AULA
BAGNO
ALLOGGIO IMPERIALE
AMBULATIO
ALLOGGIO
TRICLINIO
RAMPA ESTERNA
TERRAZZA
CUCINA
INGRESSO

6

7

1

2

3

Ischia

The largest of the Neopolitan islands consists almost entirely of volcanic rock on which luxuriant vegetation has grown, thus earning it the nickname of Isola Verde, or Green Island (its real name, of Semitic origins, means "black island"). Just as famous for its brilliantly azure sea and splendid beaches as for its therapeutic mineral waters, its main center is Ischia town. The city is divided into two parts: Ischia Ponte, the oldest, facing the islet of the Castle erected in the 15th century by Alfonso of Aragon, and Ischia Porto, the more modern and touristic area. Other interesting towns are Casamicciola, one of the most ancient and renowned thermal resorts on the island; Lacco Ameno, a swimming and thermal center famous for the Fungo (Mushroom), a characteristic reef in front of the beach; and Forio, near the large Giardini Poseidon thermal and swimming resort.

1) Ischia Ponte: the port onto which the typical houses of the fishermen look out with the Baroque dome of the Cathedral above
2) Casamicciola: fishing boats in the port
3) Lacco Ameno: the Mushroom
4) View of the port

4

1) Panorama
2) Sant'Angelo: the promontory
3) Forio d'Ischia: evocative view of the so-called "Aquilotto"
4-5) Casamicciola: views of the port and of the beach
6) Lacco Ameno: panorama and Monte Vico
7) Lacco Ameno: panorama

4

5

6

7

1

2

3

4

5

1) Forio d'Ischia: the harbour and in the background Monte Epomeo
2) Forio d'Ischia: Del Soccorso church
3) Sant'Angelo: fishing harbour
4-5) Forio d'Ischia: view of the Poseidon Gardens

Procida

The island, located near Ischia, betrays its volcanic origins in its irregular profile, in which high reefs rising from the sea alternate with broad inlets bordered with beautiful beaches and rocky promontories with tranquil hollows softened by the cool vegetation. Procida, which is perhaps less famous than Capri and Ischia but which rivals both of them for its charm and natural splendor, is a great garden of citrus trees and vineyards which have found its fertile soil and mild climate ideal for prospering and producing high quality fruit. Quiet and enchanting, the most populous town is Procida, on a tongue of earth that projects into the sea between Marina Grande (the main port) and Marina Corricella (the broad inlet between Punta dei Monaci and Punta Pizzaco). With the castle, transformed into a penitentiary, practically lost, the town's nearby San Michele church (embellished by a 17th century tapestry by Luca Giordano) is the main artistic attraction. A beautiful scenic road reaches Marina di Chiaiolella to the southwest, an enchanting inlet at the tip of which, on Punta della Palombara, are the ruins of the ancient Santa Margherita Vecchia church.

1) The port
2) The interior of the abbey church of San Michele
3) Flavius Amphitheatre: built during the reign of the Emperor Vespasian in the first century A.D.
4) The Temple of Serapis

3

4

Pozzuoli

Situated on a splendid and extremely fertile promontory facing the sea of the gulf, this small town, which has developed considerably in economic and commercial terms over the past decades, retains important evidence of the Roman and medieval ages. Pozzuoli was founded in the sixth century B.C. by colonies from Greece. In Roman times it was called Puteoli (from puteus meaning well) due to the numerous thermal springs in the area, and soon developed into an important maritime port.
As soon as we enter the town we can admire the grandiose Flavio Amphitheatre, built in the first century A.D. during the reign of the Emperor Vespasian.
With its impressive size it is the third largest Roman amphitheatre in Italy after the Colosseum and the one at Santa Maria Capua Vetere. The most remarkable part of the structure is that with the large underground parts, perfectly preserved, where the preparations for the violent combat and games took place.
The other large Roman monument in

1

2

3

1-2-3-4) Pozzuoli: Flavius Amphitheatre - details

Pozzuoli is the Serapeum, also known as the Temple of Serapis, built in the Flavi age. The large complex (75 x 58 m) has a square plan and columns, statues and precious marble decorations, and was in fact a public market. Due to the bradyseism present in the whole area around Pozzuoli the original pavement is covered by water.
The Duomo (cathedral) of the town is medieval, founded in the eleventh century and rebuilt in 1634. Recent restoration has shown that for its construction the structures of an existing Roman temple were used. It contains valuable seventeenth-century paintings.
Pozzuoli stands in the hilly area of Campi Flegrei, famous for its numerous volcanic phenomena and which extends from the area to the north of Naples to Capo Miseno and Cumae. Some of these phenomena are inactive, while others are still active. The volcanic crater of the Solfatara of Pozzuoli, the Forum Vulcani of the ancients, is partially inactive. The phase of relative inactivity, also known as solfatara, is that characterised by postvolcanic activity of emission of steam and other gases including hydrogen sulphide from which the sulphur is deposited. The large central crater, completely barren, is in fact the bottom of an extremely ancient volcanic lake which dried up in extremely remote ages, between 1500 and 1700 years ago. The so-called Bocca Grande (Big Mouth) emits vapours which can reach very high temperatures of up to 162°C, while all around the "funghiere" - strange jets of mud with a characteristic mushroom shape - mineral water springs and mofettes and emissions of carbon dioxide abound.

1

Campi Flegrei

This name (literally "burning fields") denotes a large area between the river Sebeto, Capo Miseno and Cumae. Of volcanic origins, it includes low, very fertile hills covered with vegetation and scattered with small lakes and geologically interesting areas (in particular the Pozzuoli Solfatara); on the coast are reefs and picturesque inlets.
The Romans, fascinated by the beauty of these areas, established thermal and vacation resorts here (such as Agnano and the even more famous Baia) and built grandiose monuments (like the Flavio di Pozzuoli Amphitheater), of which significant vestiges remain.

2

1) The Solfatara: detail of the crater
2) The Solfatara: boiling sands

3

4

7

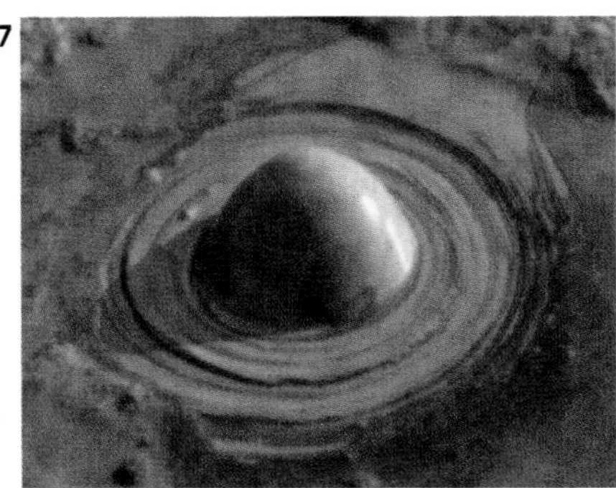

5

6

3-4) The Solfatara: details
5) The Solfatara: detail of the central crater

6) The Solfatara: evocative view of the crater
7) Bubble of boiling mud

Cumae

Together with the nearby lake of Averno which, possibly due to its stagnant and murky waters the ancients identified with the entrance to the Underworld, Cumae stands on land which throughout ancient times had for the Greeks, Romans and locals a profound religious connotation, linked to the myths and beliefs of the next world and the supernatural. Founded by the same Greek colonies of Euboea who also settled on Ischia, Cumae soon became considerably important in economic and political terms, probably as a result of its importance as a religious centre. Arriving at the site of the Cumaean acropolis from Via Domiziana, we come across the impressive Arco Felice, a monumental engineering work erected in the imperial Roman age. Twenty metres high and six metres wide, it was built to cover the crack which had been formed in the rock to allow the passage of the Via Domiziana which linked Rome and Pozzuoli. From the point on which the arch stands, the view overlooks the whole of the acropolis area, very interesting from the archaeological point of view. The famous Sanctuary is a grandiose structure excavated in the tufaceous rock for over 130 metres with a number of openings on the side facing the sea to allow illumination of the interior. The long

1

2

3

4

5

6

7

8

entrance tunnel ends in a large and evocative room with a vaulted ceiling: this is the famous Oracle Room, where the Cumaean Sybil gave out her predictions from a high and impressive seat. It is not difficult to glimpse, in the covered passage which wound in the depths of the earth as far as the oracle room the symbolic value linked to the Underworld, i.e. the next world of the ancients.

1-2-3-8) Cumae: details of the Acropolis
5) Cumae: the Arco Felice
6) Lake d'Averno
4-7) The Den of the Sybil

Sorrento

In an enchanting position on a natural terrace rising from the sea, the city enjoys an exceptionally mild climate that, along with the incomparable beauty of its hollows and small inlets opening up along the coast, have made it a renowned vacation area since Roman times. Picturesque stairways and narrow streets run through it, leading to the port and the two marinas (Piccola and Grande), framed by olive groves and citrus orchards and facing the azure sea. Immersed in its splendid garden, the Palazzo Correale di Terranova, the most important monument in the city, contains valuable works by local artisans, including the refined local marquetry.

1

2

3

4

5

1-3) Marquetry craftsmen
2) A fisherman repairing his net
4) The Sedil Dominova (16th century)
5) Panorama
6) Port and bathing resorts

6

1

2

3

4

1) Panorama
2) View of Marina Grande
3) Bathing resorts and port
4) Sedil Dominova
5) Typical carriage from Sorrento

5

2

3

4

1) Ruins of Roman Villa of Pollio Felice
2) Pompeian Villa: interior
3) Bagni Regina Giovanna
4) Characteristic view
5) The cloister of the convent of San Francesco

5

INDEX

Introduction ....pag. 4

First Part

Piazza Municipio ....pag. 6
Maschio Angioino ....pag. 8
Galleria Umberto I ....pag. 10
Piazza Trieste e Trento ....pag. 10
Teatro San Carlo ....pag. 12
Piazza del Plebiscito and Pizzofalcone district ....pag. 14
Palazzo Reale ....pag. 18
San Francesco di Paola ....pag. 24

Second Part

From Santa Lucia a Mare to Borgo Marinaro ....pag. 26
Castel dell'Ovo ....pag. 28
Via Caracciolo ....pag. 28
Villa Pignatelli ....pag. 30
Riviera di Chiaia ....pag. 31
Mergellina ....pag. 31
Posillipo ....pag. 31
Nisida ....pag. 32
Fuorigrotta ....pag. 32

Third Part

Via Toledo ....pag. 34
Sant'Anna dei Lombardi ....pag. 35
Gesù Nuovo Church ....pag. 37
Santa Chiara Church and Cloister ....pag. 38
San Domenico Maggiore ....pag. 40
San Severo Chapel....pag. 40
Piazzetta Nilo ....pag. 41
Via San Biagio dei Librai ....pag. 42
San Gregorio Armeno ....pag. 44
Cathedral ....pag. 45

Fourth Part

Piazza Bellini and the ancient Greek walls ....pag. 47
S. Pietro a Maiella ....pag. 48
Croce di Lucca ....pag. 48
Pontano Chapel ....Pag. 48
Santa Maria Maggiore ....pag. 48
San Giovanni a Carbonara ....pag. 49
Santa Caterina a Formiello ....pag. 49

Fifth Part

National Archeological Museum ....pag. 50
The Catacombs ....pag. 58
Capodimonte Museum and National Galleries....pag. 59

Sixth Part

Vomero ....pag. 65
Villa Floridiana ....pag. 65
Castel Sant'Elmo ....pag. 68
San Martino Carthusian Monastery ....pag. 70
San Martino National Museum....pag. 72

Seventh Part

Piazza Municipio and Corso Umberto I ....pag. 77
Santa Maria del Carmine ....pag. 77
Piazza Garibaldi ....pag. 78

Surrounding Areas

Mt. Vesuvius ....pag. 80
Ercolano ....pag. 86
Pompeii ....pag. 94
Capri ....pag. 102
Ischia ....pag. 108
Procida ....pag. 114
Campi Flegrei ....pag. 118
Cumae ....pag. 120
Sorrento ....pag. 122

Text: Claudia Converso
Layout: Renzo Matino - Schio
Translations: A.B.A. - Milan
Printed by: **KINA ITALIA/LEGO** - Italy